Promoting Social Cohesion through Education

Case Studies and Tools for Using Textbooks and Curricula

Edited by
Eluned Roberts-Schweitzer
in collaboration with
Vincent Greaney and Kreszentia Duer

The World Bank
Washington, DC

©2006 The International Bank for Reconstruction and Development / The World Bank
1818 H Street NW
Washington DC 20433
Telephone: 202-473-1000
Internet: www.worldbank.org
E-mail: feedback@worldbank.org

1 2 3 4 5 09 08 07 06

This volume is a product of the staff of the International Bank for Reconstruction and Development / The World Bank. The findings, interpretations, and conclusions expressed in this volume do not necessarily reflect the views of the Executive Directors of The World Bank or the governments they represent.

The World Bank does not guarantee the accuracy of the data included in this work. The boundaries, colors, denominations, and other information shown on any map in this work do not imply any judgement on the part of The World Bank concerning the legal status of any territory or the endorsement or acceptance of such boundaries.

Rights and Permissions

The material in this publication is copyrighted. Copying and/or transmitting portions or all of this work without permission may be a violation of applicable law. The International Bank for Reconstruction and Development / The World Bank encourages dissemination of its work and will normally grant permission to reproduce portions of the work promptly.

For permission to photocopy or reprint any part of this work, please send a request with complete information to the Copyright Clearance Center Inc., 222 Rosewood Drive, Danvers, MA 01923, USA; telephone: 978-750-8400; fax: 978-750-4470; Internet: www.copyright.com.

All other queries on rights and licenses, including subsidiary rights, should be addressed to the Office of the Publisher, The World Bank, 1818 H Street NW, Washington, DC 20433, USA; fax: 202-522-2422; e-mail: pubrights@worldbank.org.

ISBN-10: 0-8213-6465-0
ISBN-13: 978-0-8213-6465-9
eISBN: 0-8213-6466-9
DOI: 10.1596/978-0-8213-6465-9

Library of Congress Cataloging-in-Publication Data

Promoting social cohesion through education: case studies and tools for using textbooks / edited by Eluned Roberts-Schweitzer, Vincent Greaney, Krezentia Duer.
     p. cm. – (WBI learning resources series)
Includes bibliographical references and index.
ISBN-13: 978-0-8213-6465-9
ISBN-10: 0-8213-6465-0
1. Multicultural education—Case studies. 2. Pluralism (Social sciences) in textbooks—Case studies. I. Roberts-Schweitzer, Eluned, 1948- II. Greaney, Vincent. III. Duer, Krezentia, 1949- IV. Series.

LC1099.P764 2006
370.117—dc22
                                                 2005057739

Contents

Part I. Divisive or Inclusive? Issues in Education and Social Cohesion

Part II. Educating for Conflict or for Diversity? Case Studies

Part III. Applications

Foreword

This book is part of the World Bank's effort to understand the positive role education can play in fostering respect for diversity and to redress the potentially negative role education can play in sustaining the social divisions and prejudices that help perpetuate generations of inequity and protracted conflict. While this issue may be sensitive to pursue, it is crucial to understand the dynamics involved and to address them.

To orient itself to this issue, the World Bank sponsored a workshop in Washington, D.C., on March 24–26, 2003 on "Curricula, Textbooks, and Pedagogical Practices and the Promotion of Peace and Respect for Diversity." Under the leadership of Vincent Greaney and Kreszentia Duer, participants from multilateral and bilateral assistance agencies and nongovernmental organizations heard from presenters who related their efforts to foster respect for diversity and remove denigrating material and distortions of fact and representation in educational content and practices. Participants and country case study presenters then discussed in small groups the content of their sessions, reporting summary conclusions on interventions in curriculum, textbooks, and pedagogical practices. That work provided much of the raw material for the chapters in this volume. It also motivated the Bank's first steps to make respect for diversity part of improving educational quality and effectiveness in client countries.

It is with very great pleasure that we see this volume being made available as a resource for educators, policymakers and the development community. It addresses issues that are essential to improving the way education can shape the minds and attitudes of students. The articles address different sets of issues in different countries and regions, but the fundamental message is the same: the explicit and implicit messages about inter-group relations that children receive in school shape the form and sensitivities of young minds with respect to other human beings. If education is to contribute to economic and social development, it is critical that we understand those messages and the means of their transmission.

In a world where students will have to co-exist with people different from themselves, sensitivity and openness to diversity—ethnic, religious, linguistic, and ability-related—is a core part of any good education. Too often, preconceptions about others form the basis for misunderstandings, prejudices, fears, and violence. When countries seek to modernize or reorganize their education systems, for whatever reason, they have an important opportunity to examine what information is being transmitted, how it is being transmitted, and who is delivering it—to ensure that education serves the needs of all citizens.

Emphasizing social cohesion in education systems enhances the fundamental goal of good teaching and learning. That goal is to help every child to become a fully engaged and skilled individual who will use his or her talents for maximum individual and social benefit.

We hope that this volume will enhance the existing literature in the field and provide both food for thought and practical tools for World Bank clients and others who are seeking to improve their education systems and reduce the plight of the poor.

Frannie A. Léautier
Vice President
World Bank Institute

Jean-Louis Sarbib
Senior Vice President
Human Development Network

Acknowledgments

The Civic Engagement, Empowerment, and Respect for Diversity (CEERD) team at the World Bank Institute (WBI) would like to thank Krezentia Duer, manager of the New Practices program within CEERD, for her vision in pushing for a place at the table for education and social cohesion. Her faith and persistence made this volume possible. The team also thanks James Wolfensohn, who made sure that financing for the program was available and whose commitment to an inclusive world lay behind much of the Bank's work in this field, and Elaine Wolfensohn for her commitment to education. Vincent Greaney and other participants in the Bank's March 2003 seminar on "Curricula, Textbooks, and Pedagogical Practices and the Promotion of Peace and Respect for Diversity" did the original work for this publication. Jamil Salmi of the World Bank's Education Network and Ian Bannon of the Bank's Post-Conflict Unit have given full support for what has become a cross-departmental initiative within the institution. John Didier, Alicia Hetzner, and Steven Kennedy prepared the seminar papers for publication. Lee Joanna Harper has been the mainstay of the CEERD team, making sure we all stay on track.

Dedication

This book is dedicated to the memory of our colleague and friend Jim Socknat, in recognition of his lifelong commitment to education and his relentless efforts to promote positive values in textbooks—an invaluable contribution toward a more peaceful world.

Contributors

Maria Andruszkiewicz is a consultant in the field of children's rights, currently working as a Roma education expert on a project of the Romanian Ministry of Education entitled "Access to Education for Disadvantaged Groups." Funded by the European Union's PHARE program, the project is a follow-up to a project that ran from 2002 to 2005, for which Ms. Andruszkiewicz was team leader. Before moving to Romania, Ms. Andruszkiewicz was a program officer at Save the Children U.K., where she instigated and coordinated the "Denied a Future" project, a pan-European research project on the education rights of Roma children. She can be contacted at mandruszkiewicz@hotmail.com.

Ian Bannon is manager of the Conflict Prevention and Reconstruction Unit, Social Development Department, at the World Bank. He can be reached at ibannon@worldbank.org. Shonali Sardesai of the Conflict Prevention and Reconstruction Unit contributed the analysis of the Sri Lanka case.

Alta Engelbrecht is a lecturer in the School for Teacher Training, Faculty of Education, University of Pretoria. She is working on her Ph.D. in Education in which she compares racial representation in language textbooks of developed and developing countries. She can be reached at a.engelbrecht@gk.up.ac.za.

Vincent Greaney is an educational consultant. Formerly of the World Bank and the Educational Research Centre, St. Patrick's College Dublin, his areas of specialization include national assessment, public examination reform, and teacher education. He can be reached at vmgreaney@yahoo.com.

Jamil Salmi, a Moroccan education economist, is the deputy director of the World Bank's Education Department. He is also the coordinator of the World Bank's network of tertiary education professionals and was the Bank's official representative at the UNESCO World Conference on Higher Education (Paris, October 1998) and at the WCHE + 5 Conference in June 2003. He is the principal author of the Bank's new Tertiary Education Strategy entitled "Constructing Knowledge Societies: New Challenges for Tertiary Education." Mr. Salmi holds a Master's degree in Public and International Affairs from the University of Pittsburgh (USA) and a Ph. D. in Development Studies from the University of Sussex (UK).

Eluned Roberts-Schweitzer is a senior education specialist in the education section of the Europe and Central Asia Region at the World Bank, with responsibilities for education programs in Georgia and Armenia. She has extensive experience in other countries in the region, as well as in the Middle East and Africa. She has taught at various colleges, most recently Columbia University. She can be reached at Erobertsschweitz@worldbank.org.

James Socknat was education sector manager in the Europe and Central Asia Region at the World Bank. He died in June 2005, but his dedication to the cause of improving education in the region and elsewhere in the world, and his thoughtful and practical approach to development issues, are reflected in his chapter in this volume. He played a key role in the work done to improve the quality of textbooks purchased in Bank-funded education operations.

Alan Smith is UNESCO chair at the University of Ulster, Northern Ireland, where he has been involved in the establishment of integrated (desegregated) schools. His work has included research on education and the conflict in Northern Ireland, young people's understanding of human rights, and the development of civic and citizenship education. He has been a British Council visiting research fellow to Nigeria and Indonesia, a consultant for the World Bank in Bosnia and Sri Lanka, and a consultant for the U.K. Department for International Development (DFID) in Zimbabwe. He was a U.K. representative to the Council of Europe on Education for Democratic Citizenship and has completed an evaluation of the introduction of civic education to the Republic of Serbia, funded by UNESCO, UNICEF, and the Soros Foundation. He was a member of an OECD working group on education and social cohesion and recently completed a report for DFID on "Education, Conflict, and International Development." He can be contacted at a.smith@ulster.ac.uk.

Susan Watts-Taffe is a consultant, writer, and researcher in the field of literacy education. Her work focuses on students experiencing difficulty with reading, cultural and linguistic diversity, teachers' professional development, and school reform. She spent 13 years on the faculty of the College of Education and Human Development at the University of Minnesota, where she was a tenured associate professor. She may be reached at wattstaffe@zoomtown.com.

Introduction

Eluned Roberts-Schweitzer

Since 2003, the Civic Engagement, Empowerment, and Respect for Diversity (CEERD) program of the World Bank Institute has included a program on Education and Respect for Diversity. The program consists of a series of initiatives to promote tolerance and respect for diversity through curriculum and textbook reform and pre- and in-service teacher training. To date it has focused on ways in which Bank-financed programs can help education systems to address the needs of all students and to promote social cohesion. Activities have included information dissemination, through workshops and papers, as well as financing for pilot programs in Colombia, the Lao People's Democratic Republic, Nigeria, Romania, and Sri Lanka. These pilots are designed to put in place strategies that can be scaled up either in the pilot country or in other programs.

- In the Lao PDR, the pilot is working with a government research institute to identify the many varieties of indigenous languages so that children can be taught appropriately.
- In Nigeria, a pilot program on literacy has developed in-service teacher training methods and materials that have helped teachers use diverse cross-cultural materials to meet the needs of different students.
- In Romania, a pilot module for in-service teacher training is being developed.
- In Sri Lanka, a pilot program helped the government review textbook content for sensitive material.

Why is respect for diversity in education important? The way children and young people are educated and trained affects not only their self-perception and their views of their nation, but also their image of others. If a negative image of "others" is inculcated at an early age, particularly in systems that do not encourage critical thinking, these perceptions can exacerbate hatred and be an indirect cause of violence and war. Scholars have analyzed how education systems affect social structures. Ritzen and others (2002) support the view that equality is a major marker for economic success in a country and that specific aspects of school systems (such as school autonomy) are a major factor in pushing for economic growth, which helps to attenuate conflict. They define social cohesion as a societal, not an individual, phenomenon that includes the level of trust and understanding of shared principles among groups in a society.

Over the past decade, the reciprocal relationship between educational processes and respect for diversity among peoples has become widely recognized. Although the relationship is at its most extreme before and during open conflict (Buckland 2004), it holds true in other circumstances as well. The relation can be both positive and negative. Where it is positive, education improves understanding among people, reduces internal and external violence, and enhances the society's ability to reduce poverty. Where it is negative, however, or not appropriately managed, education can foster ethnic, economic, and other tensions.

The importance of the relationship between education and respect for diversity is recognized in the Education for All (EFA) goals set by the international community at the World Conference on Education for All in Jomtien, Thailand, in 1990, and in the Dakar Framework of Action articulated at the World Education Forum in Dakar, Senegal, in 2000. Other international conventions support the proposition that education should promote tolerance for diversity. Those conventions include the Universal Declaration of Human Rights (United Nations 1948) and the Convention on the Rights of the Child, which states that education should be devoid of discrimination and should develop ". . . respect for the child's parents, his or her own cultural identity, language and values, for the national values of the country in which the child is living, and for civilizations different from his or her own" (United Nations 1989: 29, 1c). It adds that education should prepare children in a "spirit of understanding, peace, tolerance, equality of the sexes and friendship among all peoples, ethnic, national, and religious groups and persons of indigenous origin" (29, 1d).

Important recent work in this area identifies how, in societies marked by ethnic tension, education can aggravate intergroup hostility through uneven access or denial of access, through its use as a weapon in cultural repression, by manipulating history for political purposes, and segregating students to ensure inequality, lower esteem, and reinforce stereotyping (Bush and Saltarelli 2000).

A recent volume by Sobhi Tawil and Alexandra Harley (2004) presents seven case studies of countries in conflict, exploring how those societies have reacted to the challenges of conflict and social division and how education policymakers have revised their approaches to education following conflict. Each of the seven countries studied has revisited the concept of diversity—and this in turn is reflected in curriculum development for a new era.

Except where it is misused to reinforce inequities and fan resentment, education provides a path out of poverty. For that reason, support for inclusive education systems is an important part of the poverty reduction agenda of the World Bank and other international organizations. Within the bounds of advice to sovereign states, the Bank tries to ensure that the content of educational materials and training presents a fair view of all groups within a country. These groups include minority language groups, ethnic groups, those with disabilities, and those who are otherwise economically and politically disenfranchised.

Improvements in basic education should improve the chances that education will better meet the needs of all groups, just as greater emphasis on critical thinking, less rote learning, and teachers who are better prepared to deal with the individual needs of students should create an improved learning environment. Likewise, the recent emphasis in development lending on community participation and decentralization to local levels of authority should promote self-determination and create an improved learning environment.

Unfortunately, because of political pressures that often reflect long-standing prejudices and long-simmering conflicts, the delivery of education services is not only not value free but can contain messages that encourage hate and fragmentation in communities and among countries. There is a fine line between promoting a vision of nationhood—one of the basic precepts of most education systems, although often not of educators—and promoting a negative view of one's neighbor or of a neighboring country.

It is the right and duty of every elected government to judge what is appropriate for the society's or the community's children to learn. However, just as we have become more aware in recent years of the need to promote equal opportunities for girls to gain access to education, so now we are becoming increasingly aware of the potential for education systems to divide communities and nations—sometimes unintentionally. As we reach the sixtieth anniversary of the end of World War II and realize that the world is still struggling with multiple internal and cross-country conflicts, we still have much to learn about creating environments in which individuals and societies can grow in peaceful circumstances.

This volume contains 11 chapters. Most originated as papers presented at a World Bank workshop on "Curricula, Textbooks, and Pedagogical Practices and the Promotion of Peace and Respect for Diversity," held in Washington, D.C., in March 2003. The purpose of the workshop was to explore how textbooks and learning materials, teacher training, and processes of curriculum development can contribute to peace and respect for diversity. The volume pulls together these contributions, together with other materials prepared for the CEERD program on Education and Respect for Diversity, as tools for practitioners in education to use when considering how they might change their education systems to improve social cohesion.

The list of subjects that could have been included in the volume is a long one. The relationship between education and poverty, technical issues such as teacher training and school management, language of instruction, and broader issues of diversity (such as the inclusion of individuals with disabilities)—all are important topics that merit coverage in several volumes. This volume has three foci:

- The rationale for considering how aspects of education can affect social cohesion
- Case studies that review particular country experiences with curricula and textbooks
- Practical guidelines and applications to help countries improve areas of education.

The three chapters that make up Part I of the book establish the importance of the topic of educating for social cohesion, describing not only the social and economic stakes but also the power of the mechanisms at play. Together they provide a loose framework to help countries analyze education and social cohesion issues.

The first chapter, by Jamil Salmi, revisits the author's influential work, *Violence and Democratic Society: New Approaches to Human Rights* (1993). Its centerpiece is a typology of violence that anchors an analysis of how education contributes to or is affected by various forms of violence. Salmi "focuses on the complex relationship between violence and education as an illustration of how the framework can be applied to analyze issues that are not commonly looked at from a violence and human rights perspective" (Salmi 2000, 1–2).

In chapter 2, Alan Smith emphasizes that how diversity is handled in an educational system is a marker for inequality and potential conflict in society. He then reviews some of the evidence of ways to improve education systems, in particular, teacher training and curriculum development.

Part II of the volume consists of four case studies of countries or technical issues. Vincent Greaney's overview sets the stage by demonstrating that textbooks often contain material that denigrates some groups in the eyes of others. Nationalism, religious bias, omission or imbalance in content, factual inaccuracies, and biased pictures or maps are a few of the ways in which poorly developed books can bias learning and understanding.

Alta Engelbrecht's case study on South Africa looks at the ways in which that country's textbooks have changed as government and social priorities have broadened. These changes involved not only racial stereotyping, but also linguistic and religious content. Pointing out that issues in the portrayal of history remain unaddressed, Engelbrecht underlines the importance of revising textbooks in the aftermath of authoritarian regimes.

Susan Watts-Taffe reviews the process of textbook adoption in the United States with an emphasis on promoting respect for diversity. A set of general procedures exists, from which lessons can be learned and recommendations made, but implementation of those procedures varies from state to state. The author suggests systemwide improvements for monitoring public opinion and for ensuring that local selection committees represent a broad range of stakeholders, among other issues.

In a case study that focuses on the impact of curricula on learning and integration, Maria Andruszkiewicz reviews the status of Roma children in Europe, revealing how poor and inappropriate curricula impede their learning and their ability to integrate into European societies. In many countries Roma children are still isolated linguistically and socially, and educated apart from others in special schools. The author outlines ways in which these populations can be helped to take better advantage of education systems.

Part III presents some applications learned from situations such as those described in Part II, as well as some tools for diagnosis and improvement. Ian Bannon examines the potential of social analysis for education projects financed by the World Bank, or indeed by other development agencies. Without an adequate understanding of the extent to which internal and external conflicts affect populations, interventions in education, as in other areas, will not address the needs of the population. The paper gives a framework for undertaking social analysis that can be used in any context.

In the last chapter of the volume, James Socknat provides a set of practical guidelines (for discussion by governments and international agencies) to help task managers in international aid agencies encourage careful reviews by client countries of educational curricula, textbooks, and teaching practices—all with a view to making education systems more inclusive and equitable.

The volume is a joint effort of the CEERD and education training programs of the World Bank Institute and the Education Network and the Post-Conflict Unit of the World Bank. We hope to provide educators and development practitioners with food for thought about the manner in which education systems evolve and grow, and with practical advice to help them change appropriately.

References

Buckland, Peter. 2004. *Reshaping the Future. Education and Post-Conflict Reconstruction.* Washington, DC: World Bank.

Bush, K. D., and D. Saltarelli. 2000. *The Two Faces of Education in Ethnic Conflict.* Florence: United Nations Children's Fund, Innocenti Research Centre.

Ritzen, J., Lianqin Wang, and Yael Duthilleul. 2002. "Education as an Agent of Social Cohesion."

Salmi, Jamil. 1993. *Violence and Democratic Society: New Approaches to Human Rights.* London: Zed Press.

———. 2000. "Violence, Democracy, and Education: An Analytical Framework." LCSHD Paper Series 56. Human Development Department, World Bank.

Tawil, Sobhi, and Alexandra Harley, eds. 2004. *Education, Conflict, and Social Cohesion.* Studies in Comparative Education Series. Geneva: UNESCO-IBE.

United Nations. 1948. "Universal Declaration of Human Rights." Available from http://www.un.org/Overview/rights.html. Accessed May 2005.

United Nations. 1989. "Convention on the Rights of the Child." Available from http://www.unicef.org/crc/crc.htm. Accessed May 2005.

Part I
Divisive or Inclusive?
Issues in Education
and Social Cohesion

1

Violence, Democracy, and Education: An Analytic Framework

Jamil Salmi

> Education provides people with the keys to the world.
>
> —José Martí (1853–95)

On October 21, 1989, the Berlin wall fell, announcing the collapse of the Soviet empire and the demise of twentieth-century socialism.[1] In a much-celebrated article published the same year, senior U.S. Department of State official Francis Fukuyama (1989) announced the "end of history," celebrating "the unabashed victory of economic and political liberalism and the universalization of Western democracy as the final form of human government."

Yet how do we reconcile the triumph of Western liberalism with the pictures of chaos, war, crime, terror, and poverty that continue to appear in the daily news? These disturbing images do not come only from the unruly former republics of the Soviet Union, the fundamentalist regime of Afghanistan, or the fanatic dictatorships of Saddam Hussein and Slobodan Milosevic. They originate also from the rich democratic societies of our planet. For example, in the United States, the wealthiest nation of the world, 20 percent of children live in poverty; one in four children is exposed to family alcoholism; 3.5 million people are homeless; one-third of low-income families go hungry on a regular basis; 25 million adults are functionally illiterate; 44 million citizens live without health insurance; 23,000 people are murdered, and 50,000 rapes are reported every year; and the country boasts the highest concentration of jailed people in the world. Are these staggering statistics just reflections of accidental events and crises, or does violence coexist, in a significant fashion, with capitalism and democracy? What role does education play in this context?

To begin to address these questions, this chapter is divided into three parts. First, it presents a framework that systematically compares and contrasts different forms of violence. Second, it discusses how this typology can be used along various analytical dimensions. Finally, it focuses on the complex relationship between violence and education as an illustration of how the framework can be applied to analyze issues that are not commonly looked at from the perspective of violence and human rights.

---

[1]This article is adapted from Salmi (1993).

The Different Categories of Violence

Most people think of violence in a narrow context, equating it with images of war (as in Kosovo), murders (as in Washington, D.C.), or riots (as in Indonesia). However, violence, defined as any act that threatens a person's physical or psychological integrity, comes in many forms. Four main analytical categories can be put forward to classify the different forms of violence that can be inflicted on a human being:

- Direct violence
- Indirect violence
- Repressive violence
- Alienating violence.

When people write or talk about violence, it is usually *direct violence* to which they refer—those physical acts that result in deliberate injury to the integrity of human life. This category includes all sorts of homicides (genocide, war crimes, massacres of civilians, murders), as well as coercive or brutal actions involving physical or psychological suffering (forced removal of populations, imprisonment, kidnapping, hostage taking, forced labor, torture, rape, maltreatment, battery, female circumcision). Violence inflicted during the wars and civil conflicts in such places as Bosnia Herzegovina, Rwanda, Sierra Leone, Sudan, and, most recently, Iraq are illustrations of this category of violence.

Indirect violence is a category intended to cover harmful or deadly situations that, although due to human intervention, do not involve a direct relationship between the victims and the institutions, population groups, or individuals responsible for their plight. Two subcategories of this type of violence need to be distinguished: *violence by omission* and *mediated violence*.

Violence by omission is defined by drawing an analogy with the legal notion of nonassistance to persons in danger. In some countries, there is a legal penalty to punish citizens who refuse or neglect to help victims of accidents or aggression in need of urgent care. Addressing violence by omission requires applying, at the social or collective level, a similar notion of "criminal failure to intervene" whenever human lives are threatened by actions or phenomena whose harmful effects are technically avoidable or controllable by society. For example, some historians have accused the U.S. government of failing to intervene early enough on behalf of the victims of the Nazi holocaust, arguing that the State Department had received sufficient information about Hitler's "final solution" as early as 1942 (Morse 1967). Only in January 1944, after reading the conclusions of a secret memorandum entitled "Acquiescence of This Government in the Murder of the Jews," did President Roosevelt order the U.S. Army to take immediate steps to rescue the victims of Nazi extermination plans (Morse 1967). Richard Breitman (1999) documents a similar failing in Great Britain, where Anthony Eden's government did not react to reports of mass executions of Jews.

This "violence by omission" approach applies not only to the lack of protection against physical violence but also to the lack of protection against social violence (hunger, disease, poverty), against accidents, occupational and health hazards, and against violence resulting from natural catastrophes. In countries in which resources are abundant but unequally distributed, the victims of poverty, which Mark Twain called "the greatest terror," could be regarded as experiencing violence by omission. This designation is certainly true in the case of mass hunger. In 1944 and 1945, for example, the French occupation forces in Indochina contributed indirectly to the death by starvation of 2 million Vietnamese by denying them access to rice stocks after the crop had failed.[2]

Similarly, the devastation of natural disasters can be seen as a form of indirect violence whenever it is recognized that human intervention could have lessened the impact of seemingly uncontrollable acts of nature. For example, experts have established that the Armero catastrophe in Colombia in 1985 would not have killed as many people had the Nevada del Ruiz volcano been carefully observed and the population evacuated before the fateful mudslide (Vanhecke 1985). The impact of the most recent tsunami tragedy (December 26, 2004), affecting several countries across a whole region, might have been lessened by better preparation and monitoring for this kind of disaster.

In contrast to violence by omission, which happens in a passive way, *mediated violence* is the result of deliberate human interventions in the natural or social environment whose harmful effects are felt in an indirect and sometimes delayed way. Examples of mediated violence are all forms of ecocide involving acts of destruction or damage against our natural environment. The use of the defoliant Agent Orange in the Vietnam and Afghanistan wars by the U.S. and Soviet armies was intended primarily to destroy crops in enemy territory. However, Agent Orange has caused genetic malformations among babies in the infected areas and cancer among war veterans. The sale in developing countries of pesticides and medical products banned in the country of origin is another illustration of this type of violence.

Paradoxically, embargos against repressive regimes, motivated by generous principles of solidarity with populations suffering under a dictatorial regime, also can be a source of mediated violence. The former UNICEF representative in Haiti documented the terrible impact on the children and women of that country of the UN-imposed embargo against the illegal government of General Cédras (Gibbons 1999). In the countryside, for example, many people died of common diseases because transport was disrupted as a result of the embargo on petrol.

Repressive violence refers to the most common forms of human rights violations regularly documented and monitored by international NGOs such as Amnesty International and Human Rights Watch. Violations of civil rights occur whenever people are denied freedom of thought, religion, and movement, or equality before the law, including the right to a fair trial. Violations of political rights exist in countries in which there is/are no genuine democracy, no fair elections, and no freedom of speech or association. Violations of social rights occur in countries in which it is not legal to form a trade union or to go on strike.

The notion of *alienating violence*, which refers to the deprivation of a person's higher rights, including the right to psychological, emotional, cultural, or intellectual integrity, is based on the assumption that a person's well-being does not come only from fulfilling material needs. Looking at alienating violence means paying attention to the satisfaction of such diverse nonmaterial needs as empowerment at work or in the community, the opportunity to engage in creative activities, a young child's need for affection—some child psychologists are now talking about the crucial role of a dimension called emotional intelligence—and the feeling of social and

---

[2]Reported in Zinn (1980: 461).

cultural belonging. Examples of alienating violence are found in countries with deliberate policies of ethnocide that threaten to destroy the cultural identity of an entire linguistic or religious community. In Morocco, for example, the Berbers, who comprise 60 percent of the total population, do not have official recognition in schools or in the media. Racism, and prejudicial practices against any particular group in society, such as homosexuals or the elderly, are other forms of alienating violence found in many places.

Freedom from fear is a key dimension in this discussion of alienating violence. The daily lives of millions of people throughout the world are affected by feelings of anxiety, dread, or terror. These emotions are found among communities caught in situations of direct violence, such as war, civil strife, and repression. Feelings of apprehension, or the more serious posttraumatic stress syndrome, often continue for decades after the end of the conflicts, aggravated in many cases by the presence of land mines, which lie dormant in the ground in more than 70 countries and kill or maim up to 20,000 people a year, mostly civilians (International Campaign To Ban Landmines, no date).

People living in urban areas with high crime rates also are subject to this type of anxiety. A survey among inhabitants of the largest metropolitan areas in Latin America indicates that, even in cities with relatively low levels of crime, a large proportion of people live in fear. Often, fear of crime leads people to restrict their mobility in terms of the times of day they can or will leave their houses or districts and the places to which they can safely go. The rapid growth of security products and services in both industrialized and developing countries is a sad illustration of the importance of this dimension of fear. In his Annual Message to Congress in 1941, President Roosevelt had mentioned "freedom from fear" as one of the four essential freedoms he wanted to preserve for the American people, together with freedom of expression, freedom of worship, and freedom from want.

Table 1.1 below summarizes the main dimensions of the proposed analytical framework and indicates possible levels of responsibility for each of the types of violence outlined above.

Applying the Analytical Framework for Violence

How can this framework be used? Its main advantage is that it constitutes a flexible analytical tool for investigating complex situations in a systematic, thorough, and objective manner. One can compare situations of violence along several dimensions—for example, geographical, historical, ideological, and institutional—to establish and study patterns of interconnections and causal relationships in a consistent way.

Along the space dimension, levels and occurrences of violence can be analyzed in different countries using the same methodological approach. Linkages can be found even across national borders. For example, between the look of wonder of a European child buying a first electronic game and the exhaustion in the eyes of an Asian woman who spends her day assembling tiny electronic components, there is a whole set of complex economic and social relationships. In some cases, action in the name of economic development leads to both social and environmental catastrophe. Environmental specialists have explained that the impact of the October 1999 floods in India—which killed more than 17,000 people—would have been much less deadly had the mangrove trees, which had always been a natural protection against floods, not been cut to set up lucrative shrimp

Table 1.1. Typology of four categories of violence

Category	Individual	Group	Firm	Government
Perpetrator				
Direct violence (deliberate injury to the integrity of human life)				
Murder	X	X		X
Massacre		X		X
Genocide				X
Torture	X	X		X
Rape and child sex	X	X		X
Maltreatment	X	X		X
Female circumcision	X	X		
Forced resettlement	X	X		X
Kidnapping/hostage taking		X	X	X
Forced labor (including child labor)	X	X	X	X
Slavery	X	X		
Indirect violence (indirect violation of right to survival)				
Violence by omission (lack of protection against . . .)				
Poverty			X	X
Hunger			X	X
Disease			X	X
Accidents			X	X
Natural catastrophes				X
Mediated violence (harmful modifications to the environment)		X	X	X
Repressive violence (deprivation of fundamental rights)				
Civil rights				
Freedom of thought		X		X
Freedom of speech		X		X
Freedom of religion		X		X
Right to a fair trial				X
Equality before the law				X
Freedom of movement				X
Political rights				
Freedom to vote				X
Freedom of association				X
Freedom to hold meetings				X
Social rights				
Freedom to strike			X	X
Freedom to form a union			X	X
Protection of private property				X
Alienating violence (deprivation of higher rights)				
Alienating living/working conditions	X	X	X	X
Racism	X	X		X
Social ostracism	X	X		X
Cultural repression		X		X
Living in fear	X			X

farms geared to the export market (Menon and Kavadi, no date). Along the time dimension, one can look at historical patterns of violence, outlining, for example, the causal relationship between colonialism and the growth of the Western economies. As Nobel Peace Prize winner Bishop Desmond Tutu of South Africa is often quoted as saying:

> When the missionaries first came to Africa they had the Bible and we had the land. They said, "Let us pray." We closed our eyes. When we opened them, we had the Bible and they had the land.

There often is a dynamic relationship among different forms of violence that can be mutually reinforcing. A 1999 econometric study showed, for example, that income inequality (indirect violence) has a significant and positive effect on the incidence of violent crimes (Fajnzylber and others 1999).

The same approach can be applied to compare different realities across ideological boundaries. The typology of human rights violations can be used for capitalist and communist societies, for kingdoms and republics, and for secular and fundamentalist regimes. Looking, for instance, at the defunct Soviet Union through this analytical framework, it is possible to identify the main dimensions of the human cost of socialism as it functioned in that context. The history of the Soviet regime is filled with tales of terror, massacres, mass executions, deportation of entire population groups, purges, and concentration camps, reflecting unprecedented levels of institutionalized state terrorism.[3]

The framework is helpful in identifying harmful situations in democratic societies in which, theoretically, human rights are fully protected by the rule of law. The French government was condemned by the European Court of Justice for the use of torture by police against common criminals. Amnesty International launched a campaign against capital punishment in the United States, which is one of the few countries in the world, together with Iran, Pakistan, and Somalia, in which the death penalty can still apply to people under the age of 18.

The typology allows measurement of the respective roles and responsibilities of different institutions, from individuals to groups of people, to firms, to governments, to multinational companies. For example, thousands of Bolivians and Paraguayans died between 1932 and 1935 because their nations were at war; but in reality, it was a war by proxy between two giant U.S. oil companies—Standard Oil of New Jersey and Shell Oil—competing for control of the Chaco oil fields at the border between the two countries (Galeano 1998).

A final observation concerning the application of the framework is that a particular occurrence of violence may fall under several categories simultaneously. Slavery, for example, cuts across all four categories of violence. It encompasses the direct violence of the manhunt in West Africa, the forced voyage to America and the denial of freedom, the indirect violence of the slaves' living conditions, the repressive violence inflicted on people who never had any rights whatsoever, and finally the alienating violence involved in uprooting Africans and plunging them into a totally foreign cultural and social environment and denying them their basic dignity as human beings.

---

[3]See, for example, Heller and Nekrich (1986), Conquest (1973 and 1979), Medvedev (1976), Carrère d'Encausse (1978).

Violence and Education

Can the same analytical framework be applied to the concept of education? At first sight, violence and education do not fit well together. The former refers to harmful situations that cause people to suffer; the latter to a positive process of intellectual and moral growth. In fact, the two notions, which appear to belong to very separate realities, have many points of intersection. In some countries, schools are violent environments, and the education process, or lack thereof, is an important determinant of violence. At the same time, education can be a powerful instrument to reduce violence and improve the human rights situation in society.

As early as 1948, the international community decided to include in the Universal Declaration of Human Rights an article affirming that education should be free, at least in the elementary and fundamental stages (UN 1948: Article 26). The Declaration went on to indicate that elementary education should also be compulsory. Several other texts and legal instruments have reaffirmed the importance of this basic human right—for example, the International Covenant on Economic, Social, and Cultural Rights, the 1959 Declaration of the Rights of the Child, and the 1990 Convention on the Rights of the Child.[4]

The UNESCO Convention against Discrimination in Education introduced a second, related dimension: equality of educational opportunities (UNESCO 1960). "Equality" refers to the obligation of states to offer access to education equally to all children, regardless of differences in gender or in regional, ethnic, religious, or linguistic background.

The third dimension of education as a human right defended by the United Nations system is the notion of freedom of choice. The International Covenant on Civil and Political Rights (UN 1966/1976: Article 18) states that "The State Parties to the present Covenant undertake to have respect for the liberty of parents . . . to ensure the religious and moral education of their children in conformity with their own convictions."[5]

To ensure a more systematic and thorough assessment of the relationship between violence and education, it is possible to apply the analytical framework presented earlier, looking at the linkages from two complementary angles: first, education as a place or a determinant of violence, and, second, education as an instrument to reduce societal violence.

---

[4]The Convention has been ratified by 191 countries. Only two countries have not ratified it: Somalia and the United States.

[5]To emphasize the importance attached to education as a human right, the UN Commission on Human Rights, under the authority of the Economic and Social Council (ECOSOC), has issued since 1998 an annual report on countries' degree of compliance with the right to education as defined by the United Nations system. The content of this annual report reveals a relatively cautious and restricted discussion of the issues involved. With regard to access and availability, the report usually focuses on national legislation on compulsory and free education without reviewing actual compliance. Equality of opportunity is looked at exclusively from the viewpoint of gender inequities, undoubtedly a crucial element but certainly not the only one. Unequal access deserves to be analyzed along socioeconomic, ethnic, linguistic, and religious lines as well. Finally, there is little consensus among the members of the Commission on considering parents' choice as a fundamental human right at the same level as access to basic education. Many states view it as a Western, capitalist notion designed to legitimize existing patterns of social or racial inequality or justify the introduction of voucher systems.

Education as a Locus of Violence

Direct violence. To begin with direct violence, it should be noted that schools are not always the sanctuaries of peace and harmony that they are expected to be. In many countries, societal violence reaches into the schools. The U.S. case is one of the most striking examples.[6] In a society in which gun violence is a major public health hazard, schools are not immune. In many urban schools, passing through a metal detector is a student's first daily "educational" experience. Students are not allowed to carry book bags to school. Police officers and dogs on patrol are part of the regular school landscape. The frequency of school massacres, as exemplified by the Stockton massacre in January 1989 or the Columbine High School killings in Colorado in April 1999, has increased. Nine school shootings were recorded between 1998 and 2000 across the country (Pressley 2000). A *Washington Post* poll of the concerns of American people in the context of the 1999 presidential campaign revealed that, of a list of 51 problem areas, lack of safety in schools ranked second. Financial resources that could be used for pedagogical purposes are sometimes channeled to purchase security equipment, as exemplified by a decision by Montgomery County authorities in the State of Maryland to invest close to US$700,000 to install electronic monitoring equipment in all schools in the county.

The presence of guns and knives in schools is also a major preoccupation in countries going through civil war, such as Colombia or Sierra Leone. In Nicaragua, gang violence in schools became a worrisome phenomenon, so the presence of armed policemen became indispensable to assuage the fears of parents. The University of Antioquia in Medellín, Colombia, the oldest higher education institution in the country, increasingly was under siege by armed groups from all political sides. Students lived in a state of "panic and consternation."

> The main administration building has been dynamited by leftist guerillas; a respected professor, a student leader and a popular cafeteria worker have been shot to death on university grounds for political reasons; and a right-wing paramilitary group has begun to operate openly and circulate a death list of future targets (Rohter 1999).

War and postconflict situations can have devastating effects on a school system. In 2005, 17 of the 48 countries of Sub-Saharan Africa were affected by civil strife. In countries including Afghanistan, Angola, Bosnia, Cambodia, Chechnya, Croatia, Iraq, Mozambique, Nicaragua, and Somalia, the presence of land mines in former conflict areas prevents children from getting an education because of the life-threatening danger involved in something as basic as walking from the home village to the local school. Schools have been bombed, and children have died during conflicts, in Bosnia, Iraq, Lebanon, and elsewhere. On December 17, 1999, 20 students aged 9 to 15 were wounded by shrapnel when shells fired by an Israeli-allied militia exploded in an elementary school in southern Lebanon, which has been hit five times in as many years (Mantash 1999). In Colombia, large numbers of school teachers and students have been threatened or killed by the various guerrilla and paramilitary groups, as described below.

> In the last ten years, being a teacher in Colombia has become as dangerous as being a soldier, policeman or journalist. On average, one teacher is killed

---

[6]See, for example, Salmi (1992).

every fifteen days. . . . Some teachers, who ignored the threats, have been murdered in front of their own class (Restrepo 1991: 8).

Refugees and displaced persons offer another, and different, challenge to the educational authorities of the affected countries. Additional resources are needed to provide schooling in remote areas, in which often there are no schools. Appropriate pedagogical approaches are required to help children traumatized by their exposure to conflict situations. At the end of 2004, there were close to 6 million refugees and internally displaced people in Sub-Saharan Africa.[7] In Colombia again, it is estimated that up to 15 percent of the rural population is displaced as a result of guerrilla or paramilitary activity, which means that thousands of children are deprived of a normal school experience. As a result of the civil war in Guatemala in the early 1980s, an estimated 20 percent of the overall population lived as refugees in the mountain areas of the country or in neighboring Mexico.

While less newsworthy, corporal punishment is another important dimension of direct violence that is part of the daily school experience of children in many countries, especially in the developing world. Beatings are seen in many cultures as a normal enforcement tool to motivate students to learn better, in defiance of the International Convention on the Rights of the Child, which stipulates the use of discipline consistent with the dignity of the child (UN 1989/1990: Article 28). In Morocco, for example, a majority of primary school teachers work with a ruler, a stick, or a piece of rubber garden hose that is used to hit the children (Salmi 1981). An American researcher, Vanessa Maher, who spent a year in the Moroccan countryside, recalls that teachers usually "shout their lesson, delivering ridicule and blows freely." (Maher 1974: 81). As one teacher explained:

> (T)he children have always been hit, beaten at home and in the street. If one takes up a different system in school, they become too spoiled and one cannot control them anymore. True we are taught many things at the teacher training college, everything about psychology and pedagogy, but when we arrive here, we don't know how to deal with them. Using the stick is the best way (Belarbi 1976: 49).

There is an old Colombian saying to the effect that a child can learn well only after a strong beating (*la letra con sangre entra*), reflecting an ancient tradition of school beatings that is still prevalent in the rural parts of the country. Corporal punishment and school bullying are also widespread in socially cohesive societies such as Japan. The 1994 suicide of a 13-year old boy, Kiyoteru Okochi, who had been repeatedly humiliated and harassed by other boys without intervention by the school authorities, brought this issue to international attention (Hirsh and Takayama 1994: 37). In the United Kingdom, where corporal punishment traditionally was extensive and brutal, there have been efforts to reintroduce this practice in schools, despite the European Court of Human Rights' condemnation of Britain in this regard (Parker-Jenkins 1997).

Indirect violence. Illiteracy, a strong factor of poverty, is one of the most debilitating forms of indirect or social violence. For the millions of girls and boys who are denied access to school, or who are rejected after only a few years, living without the capacity to read and write will be a serious handicap for their entire lives. Illiteracy affects their ability to find remunerated employment and become more productive

---

[7]http://worldviews.igc.org/awpguide/refugees.html

if they are self-employed. Illiteracy is also potentially life-threatening because of its negative impact on the health of its victims and their families, especially in the case of girls and mothers, who usually play the leading part in the transmission of progressive hygiene and health habits. World Bank researchers have underscored a clear correlation between girls' education and mortality rates, especially child mortality (Hill and King 1995).

The scores of children who are excluded from schools are usually the victims of negligent government policies that have failed to make "education for all" a real national priority. Some groups in society can be affected more than others. In many South Asian, African, and Arab countries, for example, girls fare systematically worse in terms of access to school and permanence in the education system. According to UNICEF, 60 percent of the 130 million children aged 6 to 11 who are not in school throughout the world are girls. In the Caribbean region, by contrast, there is a reverse pattern of gender inequality, whereby the school performance of boys is below that of girls. In several Latin American countries, children from the indigenous populations are less likely to enter school, to stay in school, or to perform well academically than the rest of the population. In Peru, for example, Quechua children score an average of 30 percent lower than Spanish speakers on national tests of academic achievement (World Bank 1999: vol. 1, p. 38). In Guatemala, according to Ministry of Education statistics, the average education level of indigenous females is less than one year of formal education, and the illiteracy rate is as high as 70 percent. In contrast, the average number of school years is 4.5 for the nonindigenous population, whose illiteracy rate is only 40 percent.

Sometimes, government negligence is compounded by deliberate discriminatory practices against "minority" groups from a social or legal standpoint. In South Africa, until the early 1990s, education policy was a powerful instrument for perpetuation of the unjust apartheid system. In 1970, for instance, less than 1 percent of the African and colored population had finished 10 years of formal schooling, compared to 23 percent of the white population. In the words of the then minister of native affairs:

> (M)y department's policy is that education should stand with both feet in the reserves and have its roots in the spirit and being of Bantu society. . . . There is no place [for the Bantu] in the European community above the level of certain forms of labor. [8]

Indonesia, Malaysia, and Sri Lanka are other examples of countries whose education policies were purposely and systematically biased against some ethnic minorities in the form of explicit or implicit quotas. In Eastern Europe, children of the Roma minority continue to be discriminated against to this day. (See "Romani Children in European Schools: Recent Experience," in this volume.)

Illiteracy is not only a developing-country social disease. Surveys in industrialized nations have shown that a surprisingly high proportion of the adult population is functionally illiterate. UNICEF estimated in 1999 that, on the eve of the new century, almost 900 million people, representing close to one-sixth of humanity, were functionally illiterate. This situation is all the more worrisome as rapid technological advances and the information and communication revolutions are drastically changing the content of jobs and career patterns. No longer a luxury but a necessity for

---

[8]Quoted in Troup (1976: 4).

survival and adaptation, lifelong education is not accessible to the relatively large share of the population falling into the category of functionally illiterate people.

In many developing countries, especially in the rural areas, the physical conditions for learning available to children are far from adequate. Schools operate without a proper sanitary infrastructure or without sufficient protection against harsh climatic conditions such as rain and heat. In rural Peru, for instance, 68 percent of the smaller schools have no working latrines, and 39 percent of the classrooms have no roofs (World Bank 1999: vol. 2, p. 101). In Northeast Brazil, a third of all schools do not have bathrooms (Waiselfisz 1999). In some countries—for example, Trinidad and Tobago—asbestos has been used in school construction, with a significant risk of harmful exposure to the children.

School accessibility is also a factor. In rural El Salvador, in the wake of floods, the number of teachers and children who drowned on their way to school increased so much that it became a national problem for the Ministry of Education.[9] In some rural areas in the Philippines, children carry ropes that are used routinely to cross rivers and avoid drowning during the daily school commute.

Repressive violence. An uneducated population is fertile ground for the denial of civic and political rights. Even in countries with a long democratic tradition, the high proportion of abstentions in key political votes, for example, in the United States and France, could be an indicator that adult illiteracy and the lack of civic education in schools are obstacles to full participation by the majority in democratic life. Successive surveys of college freshmen in the United States indicate that young people are increasingly detached from political and community life.[10] In many societies, school governance, structure and organization, and pedagogical practices do not reflect the democratic ideals that could positively affect the young people educated in these schools. As two U.S. professors emphasized in a book on democratic schools, "the most powerful meaning of democracy is formed not in glossy political rhetoric, but in the details of everyday lives." (Apple and Beane 1995: 103)

Alienating violence. The last category of violence, alienating violence, is particularly relevant to this review of education and human rights. In many education systems, there is a wide disconnect between the curriculum taught at school and the community that curriculum is meant to serve, as humorously illustrated by Charles Schulz and his "Peanuts" characters:

> "I learned something in school today. I signed up for folk guitar, computer programming, stained glass art, shoemaking and a natural foods workshop. I got spelling, history, arithmetic and two study periods."
>
> "So what did you learn?"
>
> "I learned that what you sign up for and what you get are two different things."[11]

For millions of children, being confronted with an alien curriculum in terms of content and, sometimes, language of instruction makes for a very unsettling educational experience. The language situation in Morocco offers an interesting example

---

[9]Interview with Cecilia de Cano, Minister of Education, Republic of El Salvador, October 4, 1999.

[10]Referred to in Association for Supervision and Curriculum Development (1998).

[11]Quoted in Reimer (1971: 22).

of this type of challenge. As a child, the young Moroccan learns either one of three Berber dialects or Moroccan Arabic in the family and immediate community. When children enter primary school, they begin to be taught in classical Arabic, an erudite written language that is linguistically distinct from the Moroccan Arabic spoken in the country. After two years, children are introduced to French, which will serve as the vehicle for learning mathematics and natural sciences. During these years of acquiring basic literacy skills, the mother tongue (Berber or Moroccan Arabic) is strictly banned from the classroom. Many students end up with serious shortcomings in terms of cognitive achievement, not because of inherent intellectual deficiencies but because they have to study in what are for them, from a purely linguistic viewpoint, two "foreign" languages (Salmi 1987: 21–31).

Textbooks often reflect a cultural, urban, or gender bias that misrepresents minority groups or population segments with a minority status. Studies of textbooks used in Latin America, for example, have shown that black people have been systematically eliminated from any reference outside the slavery period. Moreover, when depicted, black persons are associated with negative images reflecting profound racist prejudices in society (Arenas 1999). At times, the level of frustration of minority groups can be so high it leads to extreme reactions. In Sri Lanka, for example, it appears that the violent Tamil Tigers movement started among students disenchanted with an education system that totally ignored their minority culture.

Again, this type of curriculum problem is not confined to the developing world. The argument over how or whether to teach Darwinism and creationism in U.S. schools is an example of a hot debate in this area. The expansion of creationism in the United States is a striking example of biased teaching in an industrialized country. Over the past 10 years, school boards in many districts or counties have successfully removed any reference to Darwin and evolution from the biology curriculum in high schools (Mathews 1996). The August 1999 decision of the Kansas Board of Education to eliminate from state education standards references to Darwinism and to scientific accounts of the origin of the universe and the Earth that conflict with the Biblical version of creation has revived the national debate and raised the specter of censorship (Keller and Coles 1999). As a result of the Kansas decision, some librarians in religious schools have torn out the section on Charles Darwin in books about great scientists and labeled "dangerous" biology books with the following warning:

> Teacher beware: This book contains evolutionary statements. Use material carefully (Rosin 1999).

Another important dimension of alienating violence is the culture of fear prevailing in many school systems in which tests and examinations have become ends in themselves. When the purpose of each school cycle is solely to prepare for the next cycle, the anxiety to pass replaces the pleasure of learning. Intense competition, starting sometimes as early as kindergarten, is associated with the dread of failure and engenders worrisome phenomena. Widespread cheating has been documented in many developing countries such as Bangladesh and Pakistan (Greaney and Kellaghan 1996). In the United States, a survey among Duke University students revealed that close to half acknowledged some degree of high school cheating (Raspberry 1999). Child suicides occur in closely knit cultures in which school failure brings humiliation for the child and disgrace to the family, as in Japan and

Hong Kong. One of the most dramatic and extreme illustrations of the weight of social pressure was the murder of a two-year old toddler in Tokyo whose only "sin" was to be selected by lottery for admission to a prestigious kindergarten. He was strangled by an envious neighborhood mother whose own child had not been accepted (Tolbert 1999: 7–8). Moreover, as a result of the prevailing physical violence in U.S. inner-city schools, in European schools in low-income suburbs, and more generally in societies torn by civil war, teachers live in fear of being victimized by aggression from unruly students.

Finally, it is worth mentioning that, as in any other situation of violence, the different dimensions of the relationship between violence and education can be mutually reinforcing. In Jamaica and Colombia, for example, failure at school and growing unemployment lead young males into a vicious cycle of drug abuse and street violence.

Education as a Tool to Promote Social Cohesion and Reduce Violence

> Education makes a people easy to lead, but difficult to drive; easy to govern but impossible to enslave.

—Henry, Baron Brougham (1778–1868)

Fortunately, the relationship between violence and education is not always harmful—quite the opposite. On the positive side, education is an important instrument to overcome violence and improve respect for human rights. In societies in which direct violence is pervasive, or was until recently—for example, in countries torn by civil war such as Colombia and Sierra Leone, in postconflict nations such as El Salvador and Mozambique, and in post-apartheid countries such as Namibia and South Africa—political and civic leaders have emphasized the need to make schools violence-free and to promote peace education as key avenues for changing the value system and bringing up generations of young people to coexist more peaceably. In Namibia, for example, corporal punishment was eliminated at the end of the apartheid period, and school discipline is now based on a nonviolent approach called "discipline from within."

Ongoing experiences of education for peace and human rights in Colombia offer rays of hope in an otherwise discouraging situation of widespread violence. In the Northern Province of Bolivar, for instance, the Convivial Schools program (*Escuelas Territorios de Convivencia Social*) has adapted the traditional local figure of the *palabrero*, or mediator, prevalent in the indigenous population, to train a network of negotiators chosen from among students, parents, teachers, and school administrators whose role is to promote peaceful modes of conflict resolution in the school and the community. Set in a region of acute violence in which three different guerilla groups, various squads of paramilitary terrorists, drug lords, and the national army have been actively fighting and terrorizing the civilian population for two decades, the program has begun to transform the culture of schools in a more democratic way and to shield them relatively from the surrounding violence, even achieving the safe release of teachers kidnapped by the guerillas or the paramilitary.

In countries with repressive political systems, universities have often provided a forum for voicing criticism on important political and social issues. In many parts of the world, authoritarian governments have been seriously challenged by student protests, as illustrated by the Tianamen Square events in China (1989); or even over-thrown, for instance, in Thailand (1974) and Korea (1987).

Providing education helps young people acquire the fundamental skills and values needed to find productive employment, to adjust to changing labor market requirements over their lifetimes, and to live politically, socially, and culturally meaningful lives. Higher levels of education also result in better health and longer life expectancy. Girls' education, in particular, has high individual and social health benefits. Educated mothers establish better hygiene and feeding habits in their households, resulting in lower infant mortality. Educated teenagers are less at risk of adolescent pregnancy and sexually transmitted diseases. Girls' education is also proven to reduce fertility rates.

> In Brazil, illiterate women have an average of 6.5 children, whereas those with secondary education have 2.5 children. In the southern Indian state of Kerala, where literacy is universal, the infant mortality rate is the lowest in the entire developing world—and the fertility rate is the lowest in India (UNICEF 1999).

Experiences throughout the world demonstrate that programs specifically dedicated to children who have been excluded from the education system for one reason or another can have very positive results. To give just one example, the BRAC (Bangladesh Rural Advancement Committee) schools in Bangladesh have been successfully offering quality education to a growing number of children from low-income families, with a special emphasis on girls and disadvantaged children. In addition, in any society, keeping children in school is also the best way to eliminate child labor and the sexual exploitation of children.

As discussed earlier, transforming schools into settings that are free from physical violence is a fundamental requirement. However, it is equally important to eliminate dimensions of indirect violence in schools by offering to all children a healthy school environment that entails, at a minimum, provision of potable water, decent sanitary facilities, and a safe building.

Finally, several avenues can be used to make the formal education experience of children in schools more meaningful, with the purpose of reducing alienating violence. In several countries, far-reaching innovations have been introduced to transform the curriculum and improve pedagogical practices to provide underprivileged groups with a more empowering education. *Escuela Nueva*, for instance, is an interactive teaching and learning approach that stimulates learning among peers and the development of democratic behaviors in multigrade schools. Started in Colombia in the 1980s, it has been successfully adapted in other countries, including Guatemala and Honduras. The EDUCO movement in El Salvador, which began as a grassroots initiative in 1992 at the end of the civil war, has involved communities in the poorest districts of the country in the operation of their schools. The City of Emmaus School in Northeast Brazil is designed as a new form of education for street children, giving them the opportunity to learn to live as independent and responsible citizens.

For many children from linguistic minorities, access to bilingual education is an important factor to ensure a meaningful school experience and increase their chances of academic success. In Latin America, the education authorities in Bolivia, Ecuador, Guatemala, and Mexico have taken the lead in developing and implementing bilingual programs with appropriate education materials, adapted pedagogical practices, and qualified teachers.

With respect to the teaching of tolerance, a pioneering program in Southern California has had a remarkable impact at San Clemente High School, in which interethnic tensions among Asian Americans, blacks, Latinos, and whites led to serious incidents in the early 1990s. A course in which students are taught to identify and reject all forms of prejudice and racism—not just ethnic discrimination—significantly modified the social climate on campus (Smith 1999). Similarly, the Givat Gonen School in Israel, located in a district characterized by high levels of criminality and antagonism between Jewish and Arab youths, has pioneered an "education for peace" program that has successfully integrated children from the two communities.

Table 1.2 summarizes this discussion of the relationships between violence and education with a typology of the role played by education from both a negative and a positive perspective.

Conclusions

To understand fully the role of violence and the related extent of harm inflicted on various population groups or individuals in a democratic society, or in any society for that matter, two things are required. One must first conduct a systematic analysis of the different forms of violence in that society. Second, on the basis of that analysis, one must try to establish the patterns and relationships linking those manifestations of violence to the prevailing economic, social, and political power structures to establish accountability. The framework outlined in these pages is offered as a tool to facilitate this type of analysis.

This chapter has been guided by the assumption that violence is a multifaceted phenomenon associated with specific causes and responsible people or institutions. It also reflects a strong belief in the existence of universal human rights and the premise that the different forms of violence it discusses are sources of harm or suffering regardless of the type of society and culture one lives in and no matter one's own individual characteristics. Whether Chinese or Swiss, Muslim or Jew, woman or man, situations such as torture, hunger, illiteracy, lack of political freedom, living in fear, and lack of self-determination are hurtful. The degree of tolerance toward various manifestations of harm may differ from one person to the other, and from one culture to the other, but there are common experiences of oppression, suffering, and alienation that affect all human beings.

Education's place in the study of human rights violations is particularly important because of its potential role as either a negative or a positive factor with strong multiplier effects in either case. As discussed here, the possibility of enjoying an education and the quality of the educational experience bear on all four forms of violence. This impact was illustrated in a dramatic way by the anguished cry for help left behind by the two Guinean teenagers who were found dead in July 1999, after hiding in the landing gear bay of a Sabena airplane that flew from Conakry to Brussels. Their letter, addressed to the "Excellencies and officials of Europe," is self-explanatory:

> We suffer enormously in Africa. Help us. We lack rights as children. We have war and illness, we lack food. . . . We have schools, but we lack education.[12]

---

[12]Quoted in Hoagland (1999: B7).

Table 1.2. Violence and education: A typology

Category of violence	Manifestation of violence	
	Negative dimensions in the context of education	Education as a positive factor
Direct violence (deliberate injury to the integrity of human life)	Effects of violent conflicts Land mines Bombing Threats, kidnappings, murders	Education for peace
	Weapons in schools Corporal punishment Failure suicides	Weapon-free schools Banishment of corporal punishment
Indirect violence (indirect violation of the right to survival)		
Violence by omission	Illiteracy Inequities of access and achievement Gender Socioeconomic groups Ethnic groups Linguistic groups Religious groups	Education for all Equality of opportunity Including the excluded (minorities, refugees, displaced children) Education for life
Mediated violence	Inadequate infrastructure Lack of basic hygiene Exposure to rain and heat Asbestos	Adequate infrastructure Potable water and latrines Protection from rain and heat Harmless construction materials
Repressive violence (deprivation of fundamental political rights)	Absence of democracy in schools Lack of education for democracy	Democratic practices in schools at all levels Education for democracy (civic education, recognition of equal rights and freedoms)
Alienating violence (deprivation of higher rights)	Foreign/biased curriculum and textbooks (history, biology) Foreign language	Appropriate curriculum Education for tolerance and cultural diversity Use of mother tongue or bilingualism
	Alienating pedagogical practices	Pedagogical practices for intellectual and emotional growth
	Harassment Examinations as negative incentive	Harassment-free schools

References

Apple, M.W., and J.A. Beane. 1995. *Democratic Schools*. Alexandria, VA: Association for Supervision and Curriculum Development.

Arenas, A. 1999. "Education of People of African Descent in Latin America and the Caribbean." In *Encarta Africana*, ed. A.A. Kwame and H.L. Gates. Redwood, WA: Microsoft Corporation.

Association for Supervision and Curriculum Development. 1998. *Infobrief* 13 (June). Alexandria, VA.

Belarbi, A. 1976. "Les relations enseignants/enseignés dans la classe." Unpublished thesis, University of Paris.

Breitman, R. 1999. *Official Secrets: What the Nazis Planned, What the British and Americans Knew*. London: Penguin Books.

Camargo, Abello. 1997. "Are the Seeds of Violence Sown in Schools?" *Prospects* 37(3) (September). UNESCO, Paris.

Carrère d'Encausse, H. 1978. *L'Empire Eclaté*. Paris: Flammarion.

Conquest, R. 1973. *The Great Terror: Stalin's Purge of the Thirties*. Rev. ed. New York: MacMillan.

———. 1979. *Kolmya: The Arctic Death Camps*. Oxford: Oxford University Press.

Fajnzylber, P., D. Lederman, and N. Loayza. 1999. "Inequality and Violent Crime." Unpublished paper. World Bank, Washington, DC. November.

Fukuyama, F. 1989. "The End of History." *National Interest* 16 (Summer).

Galeano, E. 1998. *Open Veins of Latin America: Five Centuries of the Pillage of Continent*. Translated by Cedric Belfrage. New York: Monthly Review Press.

Gibbons, E. 1999. *Sanctions in Haiti: Human Rights and Democracy under Assault*. Washington, DC: CSIS Press.

Greaney, V., and T. Kellaghan. 1996. "The Integrity of Public Examinations in Developing Countries." In *Assessment: Problems, Developments, and Statistics Issues*, ed. H. Goldstein and T. Lewis. Chichester, U.K.: Wiley, 167–88.

Heller, M., and A. Nekrich. 1986. *Utopia in Power: The History of the Soviet Union from 1917 to the Present*. New York: Summit Books.

Hill, M.A., and E.M. King. 1995. "Women's Education and Economic Well-Being." *Feminist Economics* 1(2).

Hirsh, M., and H. Takayama. 1994. "The Other Side of Paradise." *Newsweek*, December 19.

Hoagland, J. 1999. "Help Us." *The Washington Post*, August 22.

International Campaign To Ban Landmines. No date. "The Problem." http://www.icbl.org. Accessed June 2005.

Keller, B., and A.D. Coles. 1999. "Kansas Evolution Controversy Gives Rise to National Debate." *Education Week*. September 8.

Maher, V. 1974. *Women and Property in Morocco*. Boston: Cambridge University Press.

Mantash, A. 1999. "Children Hurt in S. Lebanon Militia Attack." *The Washington Post*. December 17.

Mathews, J. 1996. "Creationism Makes a Comeback." *The Washington Post*, April 8.

Medvedev, R. 1976. *Let History Judge*. Nottingham: Spokesmann.

Menon, V.C., and S. Kavadi. No date. InfoChange India—Disasters: Background and Perspective. http://www.infochangeindia.org/DisastersIbp.jsp. Accessed June 2005.

Morse, A. 1967. *While Six Million Died*. New York: Ace.

OECD (Organisation for Economic Co-operation and Development). 1997. *Literacy Skills in the Knowledge Society: Further Results from the International Adult Literacy Survey*. Paris.

Parker-Jenkins, M. 1997. "Sparing the Rod: Schools, Discipline, and Children's Rights in Multicultural Britain." Paper presented at the Conference of the South African Education Law and Policy Association. Stellenbosh, South Africa, September.

Pressley, S.A. 2000. "Year of Mass Shootings Leaves Scar on U.S." *The Washington Post*, January 3.

Raspberry, R. 1999. "Their Cheating Hearts." *The Washington Post*, November 23.

Reimer, E. 1971. *School Is Dead: An Essay on Alternatives in Education*. Harmondsworth, U.K.: Penguin Books.

Restrepo, J.D. 1991. "Ser maestro: un peligro mortal [Risking your life to be a teacher]," *Educación y Cultura* 24: 8. FECODE, Santafé de Bogotá, Colombia.

Rohter, L. 1999. "College Students Warily Live, Learn in War's Shadow." *Miami Herald*, December 29.

Roosevelt, Franklin D. 1941. "The Four Freedoms." Address to the 77th Congress on January 6, 1941. http://www.libertynet.org/~edcivic/fdr.html. Accessed June 2005.

Rosin, H. 1999. "Creationism, Coming to Life in Suburbia." *The Washington Post*, October 5.

Salmi, J. 1981. "Educational Crisis and Social Reproduction: The Political Economy of Schooling in Morocco." Unpublished Ph.D. diss., University of Sussex.

———. 1987. "Language and Schooling in Morocco." *International Journal of Educational Development* 7(1).

———. 1992. "L'Amérique malade des armes à feu." *Le Monde Diplomatique*. April.

———. 1993. *Violence and Democratic Society: New Approaches to Human Rights*. London: Zed Press.

Smith, H. 1999. "Before the Violence Breaks Out." *Washington Post*, September 18.

Tolbert, K. 1999. "In Japan, Education Is Deadly Serious." *The Washington Post*, November 27.

Troup, F. 1976. *Forbidden Pastures: Education under Apartheid*. London: International Defence and Aid Fund.

UN (United Nations). 1948. The Universal Declaration of Human Rights. http://www.un.org/overview/rights.html.

———. 1966/1976. The International Covenant on Civil and Political Rights. http://www.unhchr.ch/html/menu3/b/a_ccpr.htm.

———. 1989/1990. The International Convention on the Rights of the Child. http://www.unhchr.chl/html/menu3/b/k2crc.htm.

———. 1999. Economic and Social Council. Preliminary Report of the Special Rapporteur on the right to education, Katarina Tomasevski, submitted in accordance with Commission on Human Rights resolution 1998/33. UN/ECOSOC document E/CN.4/1999/49.

UNESCO (United Nations Educational, Scientific, and Cultural Organization). 1960. Convention against Discrimination in Education. http://www.unhchr.ch/html/menu3/b/d_c_educ.htm.

UNICEF (United Nations Children's Fund). 1999. "The State of the World's Children 1999." New York.

Vanhecke, C. "Armero ne devait pas être détruite." *Le Monde*, November 30, 1985.

Waiselfisz, J. 1999. "Ambientes Escolares." Unpublished document. Ministry of Education, November.

Washington Post. 1999. "What Worries Americans." November 7.

World Bank. 1999. "Peru—Education at a Crossroads: Challenges and Opportunities for the 21st Century." Report 19066-PE, vols. 1 and 2. Washington, DC.

Zinn, H. 1980. *A People's History of the United States*. London: Longman.

2

Education for Diversity: Investing in Systemic Change through Curriculum, Textbooks, and Teachers

Alan Smith

Diversity represents a challenge and an opportunity for education. It is a challenge because policymakers and educators are called to respond to the claims of disadvantaged minorities for whom education represents a key to greater opportunity and parity with other groups in society. It is an opportunity because a society that learns to live with diversity is likely to achieve faster rates of economic growth and social development—if only by avoiding ethnic conflict. The accommodation of diversity in the educational system is also fully consistent with (and may even contribute to) the "outcome-based" educational practices that researchers agree are needed if societies are to achieve sustainable social and economic development in our globalized world.

Combined, *education for diversity* has the potential to propel growth and progress while reducing and perhaps preventing social conflict. Recent research points the way toward reaching that potential through changes in curriculum and textbook selection and, most important of all, through more effective policies on the recruitment, training, and retention of teachers.

Before turning to the topic of investing in diversity, let us first consider the forms in which diversity manifests itself in educational systems. How diversity is handled can provide valuable information about the potential for conflict in society.

Diversity, Conflict, and the Characteristics of Educational Systems

The power of diversity to promote development and mitigate conflict should be considered not only at times of crisis, but also in routine planning and development in the mainstream education sector. The three main reasons for this are that:

- Education is a fundamental right that provides an important means of protection against abuse and discrimination, partly by providing children and young people with the knowledge and skills to access their rights and responsibilities.
- Education is an essential tool for human development and eradication of poverty—an investment not only in individuals but also in social and economic development. Children rarely get a second chance at education.
- Education can be part of the problem as well as part of the solution. Policies and practice at all levels within the education system need to be analyzed in terms of their sensitivity to diversity and their potential to aggravate or ameliorate conflict.

Diversity and Social Conflict

There is little doubt that conflict retards education and development more broadly. Conflict and instability are major barriers to attaining the international community's goal of Education For All (UNESCO 2002). The stakes are particularly high in Africa (DFID 2001a). Ten of the 15 countries in Africa that require urgent support because enrollment rates are less than 50 percent are experiencing or recovering from conflict.

But it is important to avoid a simplistic view that, because so many conflicts occur in low-income countries, it is poverty that causes conflict. Duffield (2001) is among those who argue that the prevalence of conflict today is related more to issues of political transformation and globalization than to persistent poverty. Conflict in the world is not restricted exclusively to low-income countries or to those with the lowest enrollments in primary education. There are many examples of violent conflict in high-income countries with well-developed education systems. The "highly educated" are just as capable as the uneducated of turning to violence (including ethnic or racial violence). That fact emphasizes the need to look more closely at the *type* of education that is on offer and the values and attitudes it promotes.

While ethnicity is commonly cited as a major cause of conflict, many analysts conclude that ethnicity is more often mobilized and politicized by conflict than the other way around (Bush and Saltarelli 2000). One of the ways in which ethnicity may be mobilized for conflict is through education, either intentionally or unintentionally. Education may be used explicitly to promote a particular definition of national identity that includes certain groups and excludes others. It may be used as a weapon in cultural repression of minorities, by denying them access to education, or using education to suppress their languages, traditions, art forms, religious practices, and cultural values. Segregated education may serve to maintain inequality among groups within society. And textbooks may manipulate history for political purposes, particularly when government defines the "national story" (Bush and Saltarelli 2000).

More often, the process is an implicit one, whereby education contains certain values and messages about the diverse groups within society. The way in which other peoples or nations are described, and the characteristics that are ascribed to them, may inculcate attitudes of superiority. Where diversity of gender, ability, disability, language, culture, religion, and ethnicity map onto inequalities of power and status among groups, it becomes easier to mobilize attitudes of prejudice and intolerance that may ultimately lead to violence and conflict. Many of these negative practices will have a particular impact on girl pupils from minority groups who also must contend with gender-based discrimination.

In other circumstances, education can play an important preventive role by developing greater sensitivity to diversity and by raising awareness of the ways in which inequalities based on difference carry the potential for conflict.

Diversity as an Indicator of Trends in Educational and Political Systems

How diversity is handled in an educational system (explicitly or implicitly), and how that system is used by the authorities, can tell us much about the potential for conflict within a society.

The presence or absence of a political commitment to pluralism will be reflected in the way the system is structured and administered. Political involvement in operational matters, such as education appointments, deployment of teachers, and determination of the curriculum, may be indicators of the extent to which education is regarded as a tool for political or ideological purposes.

A lack of sensitivity to diversity is likely to give rise to concerns about equality. Equality concerns may arise in terms of "inputs," such as equal access of all groups to education; transparency in the allocation of resources; and the recruitment, training, and deployment of teachers. Bush and Saltarelli (2000: 9) claim that restricted access to education "should be viewed as an indicator of deteriorating relations [among] groups" and "a warning signal that should prod the international community to initiate what the World Bank would call a 'watching brief' so that it might anticipate and respond to further deteriorations."

Equality issues also arise in terms of educational "outputs," such as differences in education attainment and qualifications among groups. These differences have important consequences for equal opportunity of employment. Bush and Saltarelli (2000: 10) suggest that educational attainment is one of the ways in which dominant groups seek to maintain their privileged position within diverse societies. They cite examples from Rwanda, in which historically Catholic missionary schools favored the Tutsi minority through preferential treatment that led to employment by the colonial government; and Burundi, in which restrictions on the admission of Hutu children to secondary schools prevented the acquisition of necessary employment skills.

The identification of inequalities, whether in terms of educational inputs, such as access, or outputs, such as qualifications, requires *accurate information and reporting systems.* Where diversity exists, interpretations of inequalities will be politically and emotionally charged, and the reliability of statistics and impartiality of monitoring systems contested. These realities make it vital that a critical interaction among government statistics departments, nongovernmental monitoring bodies, and independent academic research takes place. Monitoring also may provide the basis for the development of education policies to address inequalities as a means of building greater trust among different groups within society.

Trust among groups affects, and is affected by, the way in which diversity is managed in the overall education system and its institutions, which may fall into one of three categories:

- *Assimilationist.* Single institutions operating according to the values of the dominant tradition; minority needs and interests neglected
- *Separatist.* Separate institutions, each serving different constituencies with relatively homogeneous populations; processes within institutions may or may not acknowledge broader diversity outside the institution
- *Integrationist.* Common or shared institutions with diversity represented within the population of each institution.

The extent to which government policy supports movement in any of these directions may increase or decrease the likelihood of education becoming a source of conflict.

Equally important are the dynamics *within* institutions, because the educational environment and the educational processes within the institution may emphasize different concepts of pluralism in practice.[1] For example:

"Conservative pluralism" is expressed by education environments that emphasize *similarities* among people and the view that all people share a common humanity.

---

[1]Adapted from Kincheloe and Steinberg (1999: 1–26).

Exponents may use language such as "Differences are not important" and "We have more in common than dividing us." Conservative pluralists avoid overt expression of cultural identity and regard religion as a private matter of personal conscience not for the public space. Display of religious, cultural symbols is avoided, and the workplace or learning environment is regarded as a "neutral" space in which controversial issues are avoided.

"Liberal pluralism" is represented by education environments that place more emphasis on recognizing and accepting *differences* among people. This approach may become preoccupied with "exotic cultures" and politically correct "celebrations of diversity" as ends in themselves. The workplace or learning environment may contain diverse symbols and expressions of identity juxtaposed within the same space. There may be more willingness to acknowledge difference as having potential for conflict—yet discomfort at addressing underlying causes.

"Critical pluralism" recognizes that similarities and differences exist among individuals at a personal level but also *acknowledges differences in status, privilege, and power relations among groups* within society and among societies; there is a willingness to identify underlying causes and explore possibilities for action to address social injustice.

Alongside its ideological characteristics, the *structure* of an education system has a bearing on the extent to which it promotes assimilation, separate development, or social inclusion; and each of these has different implications for tensions within the broader society. Educational *processes* within schools and other education institutions provide evidence of the way in which diversity is being managed and are an additional indicator of the dominant values within the wider society. An analysis of education structures and educational processes from a conflict perspective therefore could be an important component of a conflict "early warning system."

Diversity sensitivity and conflict potential also are the reasons that the current Education-for-All Model of Quality Education needs revision. The *EFA Global Monitoring Report 2002* (UNESCO 2002) recognizes that conflict is an impediment to the achievement of education for all. Despite this recognition, conceptually, the report treats the need for conflict-sensitive education as relevant solely at times of crisis and emergency. It evinces that bias in two ways.

First, the model of quality education presented in the report identifies inputs, processes, and outcomes (p. 81, table 2.14).[2] Under them, the report references a gender-sensitive school climate as part of quality education. However, it contains no reference to the need for educational processes that are sensitive to diversity (conflict-sensitive) as an equally important aspect of quality education.

Second, where the report focuses on "conflict and education," it is discussed not as an essential ingredient of quality education (Goal 6), but in a separate section that refers to the "special case" of education in emergency situations (pp. 122–27).

Curriculum, Textbooks, and Teachers—Fulcrums for Change

We began this chapter with the premise that although diversity can strengthen a society (for example, by making it more globally competitive), it can also become

---

[2]Model derived from Heneveld and Craig (1995), OECD/INES (2001), and Scheerens (2002), and presented in Education For All: Is the World on Track? (UNESCO 2002: 81)

the locus of conflict. To maximize the constructive social potential of diversity and avoid the destructive, policies and practice at all levels of an education system need to be analyzed in terms of their *sensitivity to diversity* and *potential to aggravate or ameliorate conflict.* These issues should be considered as a *routine* aspect of long-term planning and development of all education systems (in much the same way that we seek gender-sensitive systems)—irrespective of whether we live in a society that is relatively peaceful, has emerging tensions, is in the midst of conflict, or is recovering from conflict or other humanitarian crises.

Taking an overview of an education system means knowing its structure and its characteristics and becoming aware of how it can be part of the problem if we are not vigilant. It is not just access to education that is important, but also what is taught and the values conveyed. Therefore, assuming that the quality of education is about the personal and moral development of children and young people as well as their academic achievements and practical skills for employment, the case needs to be made firmly that quality education in *all* education systems is about education that is sensitive to diversity.

There are many levels within a system that need to take diversity into account. Possible entry points include:

- Securing political commitment (aims and purpose of education)
- Legislation and policy changes
- Structural change (decentralization, differentiation, desegregation)
- Curriculum change
- Resource-led change (textbooks, information and communication technologies)
- Pedagogy (school-based, NGO-supported)
- Teacher education (initial, in-service)
- Examination- and assessment-led change
- Parent initiatives, community links.

All these factors interrelate and need to be taken into account. In some countries, the education system will be complex, with functions decentralized and differentiated among different agencies. In other countries, there may be a single ministry responsible for everything. Taking a systemic approach, therefore, means taking stock of all these factors and making judgments about where best to invest time and energy to achieve educational processes that are sensitive to diversity.

The World Bank initiative to support education for diversity concentrates on three very specific aspects of education systems: curriculum, textbooks, and teaching methods.[3] One of the reasons for concentrating on these three is that they are normally a central part of education reform processes for which member states of the World Bank request funding. Often three key ingredients of any education reform proposal are to "modernize" the curriculum, to replace existing textbooks, and to improve the quality of teaching through improved teaching methods and investment in teacher education.

---

[3]Respect for Diversity through Education is one of a group of five World Bank programs launched in 2002 under the title Civic Engagement, Empowerment, and Respect for Diversity (CEERD).

What Works? Research Evidence

To an extent, the research evidence supports the view that these factors significantly affect the quality of education that children and young people receive. For example, research by Throsby and Gannicott (1990) on quality education as part of international development suggests that:

- Trained teachers make a difference.
- Instructional materials are the most cost-effective investment.
- Instruction in the student's mother tongue is most effective.
- Examinations are a useful way to monitor quality.
- Healthy, well-fed children learn better.
- The amount of learning time is important.
- Quality depends on good, decentralized education management.

On the other hand, lavish buildings and equipment will not necessarily raise quality, and curriculum reform, by itself, will not raise quality as much as effective implementation of the curriculum.

Later research by Pennycuick (1993: 1) on school effectiveness in developing countries identifies several "promising avenues" (improved curriculum implementation, good textbooks, at least 25 hours of core teaching,[4] and in-service education), as well as some "blind alleys" (curriculum adjustments, computers, reducing class size below 40, lengthy pre-service teacher education).

A synthesis of research studies by Letwin (1993) on achievement in development settings suggests that teacher salaries, teacher motivation, time spent on preparation, high expectations of pupils, and quality of texts are important. Less important are class size, school buildings, multiple shifts, and repetitions.

There appear to be consistent messages emerging from these research studies about the importance of curriculum, textbooks, and the role of the teacher. More important, it is the combined effect of these three elements that is significant—because they are interrelated. Curriculum specifies not just content, but also learning outcomes; and a key message is that *most attention should be given to effective implementation rather than curriculum change as an end in itself.* In many countries, the most tangible expression of curriculum is through textbooks, and in many developing countries a single textbook *is* the curriculum. However, the curriculum and textbooks are also mediated by teachers, and it is often teacher skills that determine the quality of learning experiences. Teacher competence in a range of pedagogies and teaching methods is an important ingredient.

Reasons for Curriculum Change—Anticipating Trends

Countries seek to change curriculum for many reasons. These may be economic (due to structural adjustment, rebuilding after financial collapse); modernization (replacing old content with new or changing the type of curriculum); political transition (new ideologies, new forms of government); reconstruction and reconciliation (after conflict); or as part of an investment in human development (the case in

---

[4]Twenty-five hours of full-time education per week including an emphasis on literacy and numeracy.

many low-income countries in which education is seen as the main tool). In most cases, there is a combination of factors.

Recent research by Parker, Ninomiya, and Cogan (1999: 117–45) suggests that the search for relevance is an important factor in motivating curriculum change. In investigating what future elements might be required for a multinational curriculum, the research team identified global trends likely to have a significant impact on the lives of people over the next 25 years, the characteristics required of individuals to cope with and manage those trends, and education strategies needed to develop the desired characteristics.

Significant future trends identified by the research include the following, several of which clearly hold the potential for increasing diversity within societies and presenting opportunities for conflict:

- Economic growth will be fueled by knowledge (ideas, innovations, and inventions) more than natural resources.
- Conflicts of interest between developed and developing countries will increase.
- Migration flows from poor to rich areas within and among countries will have an impact on security and social order.
- Economic gaps among people within countries will widen significantly; poverty will increase.
- The cost of obtaining adequate water will increase due to population growth, deforestation, and environmental deterioration.
- Increased use of genetic engineering will pose complex ethical questions.
- Information technologies will dramatically reduce the privacy of individuals.

Among the characteristics of citizens that are likely to be helpful in coping with these trends, Parker, Ninomiya, and Cogan identified the following:

- Ability to conceive of problems in global as well as local terms
- Ability to cooperate with others and take responsibility
- Ability to understand, accept, appreciate, and tolerate cultural differences
- Capacity to think critically and systematically.

The most significant educational strategy suggested to develop these characteristics is a move toward curricula that have a global as well as local dimension, as well as curricula based on "learning outcomes," as described in the next section.

The Nature of Curriculum—Informational Content or Skill-Building?

The very nature of curriculum needs to be considered carefully. During the 1980s, there was a significant move away from school-based control of the curriculum toward centralized, national curricula. However, once again, the extent to which curriculum needs to be rooted in prescribed content is being questioned.

For one thing, when curriculum is conceived narrowly as the transmission of knowledge from one generation to the next, it also may be perceived as an extremely powerful tool to promote particular political ideologies, religious practices, or cultural values and traditions. There is also the problem that, if the curriculum is conceived as simply transmission of factual knowledge, the pressure to include more and more content will increase.

The rate at which knowledge is increasing, complaints about curriculum overload, the desire to avoid a curriculum biased toward one or another group, and the need for more transferable skills add weight to arguments that have led education policymakers in many countries to advocate approaches that emphasize the development of generic skills, such as the ability to draw on multiple sources of information and evaluate conflicting evidence, and the development of media literacy, critical thinking, and social and moral development. These are the type of transferable and adaptable life skills that today's children will need in the rapidly changing world and work environments of the future. They are also likely to encourage greater sensitivity to diversity.

The rationale for moving toward skills-based curricula suggests it has a number of advantages:

- Less prescribed content means that the curriculum does not need continual updating and that teachers have more flexibility to determine how to develop generic skills across disciplinary lines.
- Inquiry-based curricula encourage problem-solving and skills development.
- Critical thinking increasingly is seen as necessary to challenge abuse of power.
- Participatory pedagogy is seen as a key element in democratization.

Implications of a Skills-Based Curriculum for Learning Resources and Textbooks

The move toward a skills-based curriculum has implications for learning resources and textbooks. The following brief examples illustrate some of these:

The operation of a *single textbook policy* may offer a Ministry of Education a way of guaranteeing a "minimum entitlement" for all pupils to basic learning resources, particularly important in low-income countries and where equal access needs to be demonstrated. However, questions may arise about who controls or benefits from the production of textbooks and about their content.

In contested societies, arguments over *textbook content* can become cultural and ideological "battlegrounds." For example, part of the education reforms in Bosnia has involved the removal of "offensive material" from history textbooks.[5] Such a process necessarily raises sensitive issues about the judgment of what might be considered offensive and by whom, about who should be involved in such a process, and how it is implemented.

The production of *single textbooks for different linguistic communities* also can present difficulties. For example, textbooks produced by Sinhalese authors in Sri Lanka have been translated to produce copies for Tamil pupils. However, the Tamil Teachers' Union identified inaccuracies in the translated versions and claimed cultural bias in some of the illustrations and content matter. This has led to demands for greater involvement of Tamil authors in textbook production.

Education reforms that promote a change from content-based syllabi to a "learning outcomes" model have significant implications for learning resources. Drawing on a variety of texts and incorporating the use of different media and new technologies may contribute toward the development of multiple perspectives. On the other

---

[5]See, for example, UNESCO (2003) for an overview of UNESCO's role in the revision and review of textbooks and learning materials.

hand, these particular reforms have an economic cost, and this broader approach requires different skills from the teacher than simply teaching from a textbook.

Implications of a Skills-Based Curriculum for Teachers and Teaching Methods

Any education strategy that seeks to develop more sensitivity to diversity must take account of the central role of teachers. Teachers mediate the curriculum and the values it conveys. The extent to which they can guide students toward productive lives in a diverse, conflict-free society will depend on several factors.

A "learning outcomes" curriculum provides opportunities to develop critical thinking but also poses commensurate challenges in the teaching skills it requires and the controversial issues that must be addressed as part of the teaching and learning process.

Whether teachers are able to rise to those challenges will, in turn, depend on recruitment policies, teacher education, and the overall status of teaching in society.

Diversity-sensitive recruitment and deployment policies include ensuring an adequate recruitment of male and female teachers from different ethnic groups and an adequate supply of teachers to provide education to different groups in their first languages. Incentives, such as housing, may be offered to encourage the deployment of teachers in underserved areas, often rural.

The quality of initial teacher education and type of training are crucial. The extent to which teachers are trained in the basics of human rights education, and the extent to which personal values and perspectives are challenged, may be important. A related issue is whether it is helpful to provide teacher education through separate, faith-, or language-based institutions.

The social status of teaching—as reflected in entry qualifications, rates of pay, and terms and conditions of employment—will affect morale and motivation.

The move to skills-based curricula, defined in terms of learning outcomes rather than knowledge content, requires teachers who are more than "subject specialists." The characteristics of teachers likely to be successful in mediating this type of curriculum include those who have:

- Basic training in rights and responsibilities
- An interdisciplinary awareness of social, cultural, civic, political, legal, economic, environmental, historical, and contemporary affairs
- Disposition to interdisciplinary learning
- Commitment to inquiry-based learning
- Skill in facilitating experiential learning
- Ability to draw on multiple resources
- Confidence in addressing controversial issues
- Sensitivity to emotional dimensions of learning
- Ability to assess student learning outcomes.

In a typical classroom lesson, teachers rarely use a single pedagogical strategy. They commonly employ multiple strategies in any single classroom session. Furthermore, the literature on teaching suggests that multiple teaching strategies enhance student learning (Rosenshine and Stevens 1986; Brophy 1990; Stanley 1991). Considerable research, particularly from Canada and the United States, demonstrates that the traditional expository strategies frequently are ineffective, for example, in teaching civic education across a broad range of students (Patrick and

Hoge 1991; Dynesson 1992). Yet, expository strategies often remain the dominant form of teaching.

Osborne (1991) suggests that effective teachers adopt *democratic styles of teaching* and share nine principles in common:

- Teachers have a clearly articulated vision of education.
- The material being taught is worth knowing and is important.
- Material is organized as a problem or an issue to be investigated.
- Careful, deliberate attention is given to teach thinking within the context of valuable knowledge.
- Teachers are able to connect the material with student knowledge and experience.
- Students are required to be active in their own learning.
- Students are encouraged to share and to build on one another's ideas.
- Theoretical and practical are established between the classroom and the outside world.
- Classrooms are characterized by trust and openness so that students find it easy to participate.

Reducing Conflict While Promoting Diversity and Social Justice: New Programs, New Teachers

Globalization has made most societies of the world more diverse and in many cases more unequal and thus more prone to conflict. Educators have been called upon, and in many cases have volunteered, to meet those challenges through innovative and interdisciplinary programs. Making those programs work, however, will require major changes in policy for the selection, training, deployment, and retention of teachers.

Educational Programs for the Prevention of Conflict

Areas relevant to the preventive role that education might play in terms of conflict come with many different labels and emphases. During the 1990s, UNESCO became preoccupied with trying to draw together these disparate areas under the common label of a "culture of peace." However, this approach has been criticized for being too eclectic and unfocused, with too much energy devoted to securing agreement on definitions.

A recent UNICEF paper defines peace education in broad and inclusive terms, emphasizing its preventive role:

> Peace education in UNICEF refers to the process of promoting the knowledge, skills, attitudes and values needed to bring about behavior changes that will enable children youth and adults to prevent conflict and violence, both overt and structural (Fountain 1999).

The UNICEF paper emphasizes the view that peace education is an essential component of quality basic education and should be part of formal education in all countries. The paper also acknowledges difficulties in terminology and points to a variety of terms used in its country and regional offices such as "education for peace" (Rwanda), "education for social harmony" (Sri Lanka), and "values for life" (Egypt).

The diversity of practice and eclectic range of peace-education initiatives can be confusing. However, in terms of their emphasis, most peace-education programs appear to fall within the following broad categories:

Skills-based programs, often labeled as "peace education," involve workshops in communication skills, interpersonal relations, and conflict-resolution techniques. It is not always clear in implemented programs how the development of *interpersonal* skills in conflict resolution might affect the dynamics of *intergroup* conflict.

Multicultural and *intercultural education* emphasizes learning about diversity and concepts such as mutual understanding and interdependence. It has been suggested that such programs fall short of their aspiration to generate more harmonious relationships within society because they "abandon the crucial issues of structural inequality and differential power relations in society" (McCarthy 1991: 313).

Human rights education focuses on universal values, concepts of equality and justice, and the responsibilities of states. Few advocate the teaching of human rights as a separate subject, but it has proven difficult to integrate it into the curriculum and other school activities. One difficulty lies in the absence of a human rights dimension in initial teacher education. Other difficulties include lack of commitment at the political level—because of the challenges that human rights education might raise for existing legislation, and because of conflicts with existing political, economic, social, religious, and cultural practices.

Civic education, citizenship, and *education for democracy* place their emphasis on the roles and responsibilities of the individual in society. During the 1990s, the number of formal democracies in the world increased from 76 (46.1 percent) to 117 (61.3 percent) (Print 1999: 7–20), a trend that has been described as the "third wave of democracy." This wave was related to significant world events such as the fall of the Berlin Wall, the democratization of former communist states in Eastern Europe, the disintegration of the Soviet Union, and the ending of apartheid in South Africa. It was accompanied by renewed development of civic and citizenship education programs, reconceptualized to emphasize principles of democracy and participation. Modern civics programs go beyond simple "patriotic" models of citizenship that require uncritical loyalty to the nation state. By defining citizenship in terms of human rights and civic responsibilities, they attempt to decouple the concept of "citizenship" from that of "nationality" to make it more difficult to mobilize political conflict around identity issues (Council of Europe 2000).

Education for international development emphasizes the interdependence of different peoples and societies in political, economic, social, and cultural terms. The relevance of such programs for the prevention of conflict has been heightened by the impact of globalization and the events of September 11, 2001. The Cold War era was characterized as one of peace and security through "deterrence." Since the September 11 attacks and subsequent events in Afghanistan and Iraq, the link between global security and development assistance has been highlighted.

Individually, none of these education programs offers a magic solution for the prevention of conflict. But together, as a complex matrix of education initiatives that address key themes and values, they could have a preventive effect in the long term. It is unrealistic to expect that such programs will have immediate impact. Nor is it reasonable to expect that nonspecialist aid managers will be familiar with the intricacies and claimed "efficacy" of individual programs (although see the chapter by James Socknat in this volume).

It may be more realistic to adopt an audit approach, one that encourages education authorities to take stock of educational provision, with a special focus on features that could have a role in preventing conflict. The absence of "key themes" might then become part of a broader debate about curriculum development strategy within the education system.

Diversity-Sensitive Education—Implications for Teachers

Cochran-Smith (2004) argues that an inescapable "demographic imperative" is leading toward greater diversity within populations. Gay (2000) finds, however, that the growing diversity of student populations has not been matched by commensurate changes in the teaching corps, which remains relatively homogeneous. Both writers find growing inequality—in Cochran-Smith's words, "marked disparities in educational opportunities, resources, and achievement among student groups [who] differ from one another racially, culturally, linguistically and socioeconomically" (2004: 4).

Cochran-Smith goes on to suggest (2004: 143–49) that teacher education that is sensitive to diversity and committed to reducing disparities will explicitly or implicitly address eight key questions:

The *diversity* question asks how the challenge of an increasingly diverse student population should be understood. Previous approaches that address diversity as a *deficit* (such as lack of proficiency in the language of instruction) have been criticized. Rather, the challenge appears to be how best to draw on diversity as a teaching and learning *resource* and avoid assimilative approaches.

The *ideology* question asks, "What is the purpose of schooling, and the role of public education in a democratic society?" It questions the values and assumptions on which education policy and practice are based.

The *knowledge* question asks, "What knowledge and beliefs are necessary to teach diverse populations?" Debate may center on the extent to which knowledge of different cultures and traditions is necessary beyond traditional subject knowledge and the extent to which teachers understand their own culture.

The *teacher learning* question asks, "How do teachers learn to teach for diversity?" It is suggested that moving from concepts of "training" toward developing skills of inquiry is helpful.

The *practice* question asks, "What pedagogical skills are helpful?" It refers to documented case studies of "culturally responsive teaching." Cochran-Smith identifies six "principles of pedagogy" that are sensitive to diversity and address inequality in practice:

- Develop inquiry-based, "communities of learners" that have high expectations of students and teachers to address problematic questions set by themselves.
- Build on what students bring to school with them—knowledge and interests, cultural and linguistic resources.
- Teach the skills necessary for new learning and bridge the gaps between what it is assumed children know and what they actually know.
- Work with individuals, families, and communities by drawing on family histories, stories, and traditions; demonstrate respect for students' family and cultural values.

- Diversify forms of assessment; it is widely recognized that most standardized testing practices perpetuate inequities and limit opportunities for poor children.
- Encourage critical thinking by including the discussion and investigation of inequity and injustice as part of the curriculum.

The *outcomes* question asks, "What should be the outcomes of teacher education for diversity?" It points to the shift toward the assessment of outcomes in terms of performance-based standards, rather than program impacts. In practical terms, this shift suggests that improvements in achievement for disadvantaged or previously excluded groups should be discernible.

The *selection* question asks, "Who should be recruited and selected as teachers?" It seems clear that teachers should reflect the diversity that exists within wider society, thereby being role models with whom children can identify and that those recruited to teach have the qualities and dispositions consistent with respect for diversity and the skills of critical inquiry. Experienced teachers may have more to offer in difficult teaching environments.

The *coherence* question asks, "To what extent is the approach to teacher education consistent across the areas identified above?" Contradictions and anomalies inevitably undermine even systemic commitments to teacher education that respects diversity.

The foregoing questions have significant implications for teacher education. For example, a country of 5 million people with one-fifth of its population in full-time education will have a student population of 1 million. At a pupil-teacher ratio of 40 to 1, such a system will require at least 25,000 serving teachers and an initial teacher system of perhaps 40 teacher educators producing at least 1,000 newly qualified teachers per year. Various factors such as geographic location of schools, difficulties in teacher supply and retention, subject specialization, and diversity of school types mean that these figures are likely to be underestimates.

Although teacher education alone cannot transform society's inequities, the potential to influence the knowledge, skills, and values that are learned by significant numbers and successive generations of the population cannot be ignored.

Conclusion—The Critical Role of Teachers

Clearly, in educational development processes, the relations among curriculum, textbooks, and teaching methods are important, but the role of teachers stands out as particularly crucial. Investments in teachers and teacher education need to be made in a systemic way that appreciates the interrelationship among the political, structural, and practice aspects of the education system. For example, more diversity in the recruitment of teachers is unlikely to have the desired impact if there is a lack of political commitment to retaining teachers through adequate pay and conditions. Similarly, it is probably a mistake to think that diversity-sensitive pedagogy can be addressed simply as a technical issue or divorced from the political environment in which it takes place. These are complex issues. Nonetheless, the potential of investments in teachers and teacher education appears critical for social and economic development that values diversity as a necessary resource rather than a source of conflict or threat to peace and stability.

References

Bardhan, P. 1997. "Method in the Madness? A Political Economy Analysis of the Ethnic Conflicts in Less-Developed Countries." *World Development* 25 (9).

Berdal, M., and D. Malone. 2000. *Greed and Grievance: Economic Agendas in Civil Wars*. Boulder, CO: Lynne Rienner.

Brophy, J. 1990. "Teaching Social Studies for Understanding and Higher Order Applications." *Elementary School Journal* 90: 351–417.

Burnside, C., and D. Dollar. 1997. "Aid, Policies, and Growth." *World Bank Policy Research Working Paper 1777*.

Bush, K. D., and D. Saltarelli. 2000. *The Two Faces of Education in Ethnic Conflict*. Florence: United Nations Children's Fund, Innocenti Research Centre.

Cochran-Smith, M. 2004. *Walking the Road: Race, Diversity, and Social Justice in Teacher Education*. New York and London: Teachers College Press, Columbia University.

Coletta, N.J., and M.L. Cullen. 2000. *Violent Conflict and the Transformation of Social Capital: Lessons from Cambodia, Rwanda, Guatemala, and Somalia*, World Bank.

Council of Europe. 2000. "Education for Democratic Citizenship." http://www.coe.int/T/E/Cultural_Co-operation/education/E.D.C/.

Department for International Development. 2001. *The Causes of Conflict in Sub-Saharan Africa. Framework Document*. London.

———. 2001. *Children Out of School*. Issues Paper. London.

Duffield, M. 2001. *Global Governance and the New Wars*. London: Zed.

Dynesson, T. 1992. "What's Hot and What's Not in Effective Citizenship Instruction." *The Social Studies*. September/October, 197–200.

Fountain, Susan. 1999. Peace Education in UNICEF. New York: UNICEF. Available at http://www.unicef.org/girlseducation/files/PeaceEducation.pdf. Accessed May 2005.

Gay, G. 2000. *Culturally Responsive Teaching: Theory, Research, and Practice*. New York: Teachers College Press.

Georg Eckert Institute. 1999. *Guidebook on Textbook Research and Textbook Revision*. Paris: UNESCO.

Heneveld, W., and H. Craig. 1995. *Schools Count: World Bank Project Designs and the Quality of Primary Education in Sub-Saharan Africa*. World Bank Technical Paper 303.

Kincheloe, J., and S. Steinberg. 1999. *Changing Multiculturalism*. Milton Keynes, UK: Open University.

Kreimer, A., J. Eriksson, R. Muscat, M. Arnold, and C. Scott. 1998. *The World Bank's Experience with Post-Conflict Reconstruction*. World Bank.

Letwin, K. 1993. "Education and Development: The Issues and the Evidence." Serial 6. DFID, London. Formerly available at http://www2.dfid.gov.uk/.

McCarthy, C. 1991. "Multicultural Approaches to Racial Inequality in the United States." *Oxford Review of Education* 17(3), 301–16.

OECD/INES. 2001. *Education at a Glance.* Paris: OECD.

Osborne, K. 1991. *Teaching for Democratic Citizenship.* Toronto: Our Schools.

Parker, W. C., A. Ninomiya, and J. Cogan. 1999. "Educating World Citizens: Toward Multinational Curriculum Development." *American Educational Research Journal* 36(2).

Patrick, J., and J. Hoge. 1991. "Teaching Government, Civics, and the Law." In J. Shaver, ed. *Handbook of Research on Social Studies Teaching and Learning.*

Pennycuick, D. 1993. *School Effectiveness in Developing Countries.* Serial 1. London: DFID.

Print, M. 1999. "Civics and Values in the Asia Pacific Region." *Asia Pacific Journal of Education* 20(1).

Rosenshine, B., and R. Stevens. 1986. "Teaching Functions." In M. Whitrock, ed., *Handbook of Research on Teaching.* New York: Macmillan.

Scheerens, J. 2002. "Improving School Effectiveness." *Fundamentals in Educational Planning* 68. Paris: UNESCO-IIEP.

Shaver, J., ed. *Handbook of Research on Social Studies Teaching and Learning.* New York: Macmillan.

Smith, A., and T. Vaux. 2003. *Education, Conflict, and International Development.* London: Department for International Development (DFID).

Stanley, W. 1991. "Teacher Competence for Social Studies." In J. Shaver, ed. *Handbook of Research on Social Studies Teaching and Learning.*

Throsby, C.D., and K. Gannicott. 1990. "The Quality of Education in the South Pacific." *Pacific Economic Bulletin.* June. Formerly available at http://www2.dfid.gov.uk/.

UNESCO. 1999. *UNESCO Guidebook on Textbook Research and Textbook Revision.* Paris.

———. 2002. *EFA Global Monitoring Report. Education For All: Is the World on Track?* Paris. http://www.unesco.org/education/efa/index.shtml > EFA monitoring.

———. 2003. "Textbooks and Learning Materials Respecting Diversity: Components of Quality Education that Can Foster Peace, Human Rights, Mutual Understanding, and Dialogue—An Overview of UNESCO's Role in the Revision and Review of Textbooks and Learning Materials." Section of Education for Universal Values, Division for the Promotion of Quality Education, Education Sector, UNESCO, Paris. Available at http://www1.worldbank.org/education/social_cohesion/doc/unesco%20OVERVIEW-%20WB%20meeting-March%2003.pdf. Accessed May 2005.

World Education Forum, Dakar, April 26–28, 2000. *Final Report.* Paris: UNESCO.

Part II

Educating for Conflict
or for Diversity?
Case Studies

3

Textbooks, Respect for Diversity, and Social Cohesion

Vincent Greaney

Formal education is designed to transmit more than basic skills like numeracy and literacy; it should also transmit key social and cultural values. The school curriculum, and the way it is taught, are expected to promote among young citizens both a sense of national solidarity and a well-informed, tolerant understanding of others. Education is a key vehicle for forming individual attitudes about other groups, both domestically and in other countries; education also helps shape a student's fundamental attitudes toward society.

The modern ideal of using the formal education system to promote more tolerance and respect for diversity has its roots in the 1948 document, "The Universal Declaration of Human Rights." The 1989 Convention on the Rights of the Child goes further, stating that formal education should not only be devoid of discrimination but also should seek to develop "respect for the child's parents, his or her own cultural identity, language and values, for the national values of the country in which the child is living, and for civilizations different from his or her own" (United Nations 1989: 29, 1c). Ratified by all but two member countries, the 1989 convention holds in addition that children should be educated in a "spirit of understanding, peace, tolerance, equality of the sexes and friendship among all peoples, ethnic, national, and religious groups and persons of indigenous origin" (29, 1d).

The Importance of Textbooks

The sheer amount of time students devote to textbooks underscores their importance. One study reported that U.S. secondary-school teachers devote three-quarters of their classroom time to textbooks; textbooks also account for 90 percent of homework time (Apple 1991). Books have an especially crucial role to play in developing countries, where teachers' mastery of subjects may be weak and teachers themselves may have no access to national curriculum documents (Greaney 1996). Indeed, access to textbooks has been identified as one of the most effective ways that schools can raise academic achievement (Hanushek 1995; Heyneman and Loxley 1983; Lundberg and Linnakyla 1992).

The presence of even a small amount of biased reading material can be a problem since reading material can contribute to the development of stereotypical negative attitudes, especially when it confirms unjustified perceptions held by others. Young people are exposed to versions of history at an age when they are most impressionable. Textbooks, in particular, have helped promote highly idealized views of one nation or group of people. At the same time, they have helped promote incorrect and inappropriate images about others, both of which may be detrimental to establishing social cohesion, respect for diversity, tolerance, and, ultimately, peace. In some instances, the tone and content of these textbooks have helped foster distrust and hatred of others as well as promote narrow ethnocentric attitudes.

The beliefs, perceptions, and understandings that students acquire early on tend to influence what they learn later in school and elsewhere (Epstein 1997; Seixas 1993). In some instances, the perceptions or understandings that they acquire of "other" groups can have far-reaching consequences, as existing beliefs tend to influence actions (Cornbleth 2002). Group-centered or ethnocentric historical views can pose serious dangers when they characterize other human beings—who belong to different groups or espouse different religious beliefs or hail from other cultures or nations—as "deeply inferior, immoral, or even subhuman" (Hamburg 1984: 8). Children fed on excessively nationalistic material from history textbooks may develop an exaggerated sense of their nation's importance and a corresponding disregard for other nationalities and political systems. Many grow up to become adults who never outgrow their basic ethnocentrism (Farr 1986).

In both developed and developing countries, textbook publishers have tended to devote insufficient attention to the positive and negative roles that reading materials play in framing young people's attitudes toward others. Although most textbook content does *not* promote material that fosters inappropriate views of others, some materials, especially history textbooks, promote versions of history and views that have the potential to undermine social cohesion.

Peace, tolerance, and understanding have been conspicuously absent in many parts of the world. In 2000, 24 of the 40 poorest countries in the world were in the midst of armed conflict or had only recently emerged from it (United Kingdom 2000). In 2001, 18 Sub-Saharan countries were directly or indirectly involved in war (Mills 2002), most of them internal conflicts. Of the 107 wars waged from 1992 to 2002, 93 were civil wars (Colletta 2002).

War destroys infrastructure and displaces people. It ravages economies. Above all, it takes lives and devastates the lives of untold numbers of survivors. Children suffer disproportionately (UNICEF 1996). During World War II, about half of Hungary's primary schools and 60 percent of its secondary schools were damaged by bombing and shelling (Romsics 1999). Much more recently, war destroyed close to half of Mozambique's primary schools. In Rwanda two-thirds of the country's teachers either died or emigrated; the economy was devastated and more than 300,000 children were killed. In Europe, the recent war in Kosovo destroyed or severely damaged more than half the school buildings (Sommers and Buckland 2004). UNICEF estimates that in a six-month period (March–August 2002) approximately 1,760 schools were damaged in Palestinian territories (Watchlist 2002). Israeli students, educational institutions, and buses have likewise been attacked by Palestinian groups. Sri Lanka's civil war led to the destruction of hundreds of schools; the presence of land mines made many others inaccessible.

In the decade of 1992–2002, war killed 2 million children, left 6 million injured or disabled, rendered 12 million homeless, traumatized 10 million, and orphaned or separated from their families more than 1 million. In 30 countries more than 10 percent of the population was displaced because of conflict (Bush and Saltarelli 2000). And in more than 30 countries upwards of 300,000 children (120,000 in Sub-Saharan Africa) were engaged as child soldiers (Bellamy 2001; Mungoven 2001). Their formal education by necessity ended prematurely (Machel 2000).

The Millennium Development Goal calling for universal primary education by 2015 is not likely to be achieved by as many as 32 countries (Matsuura and others 2001). Of these countries, 11 have been mired in conflict and face the additional burden of rehabilitating and educating war orphans and child soldiers. War's massive direct and indirect costs limit funding for education; both India and Pakistan, for instance—countries with high rates of illiteracy and low school participation—devote more of their annual budgets to military expenditures than to the health and education sectors combined.

In this chapter, we review the role education has played, or failed to play, in promoting cohesive and tolerant societies. Also addressed are the influence of the textbook in promoting nationalism, evidence in textbooks of religious or historical biases, and how textbooks deploy language and art to influence young readers. We conclude with an analysis of key issues and offer suggestions for ensuring that textbook content promotes respect for diverse and cohesive societies, and, ultimately, tolerance and peace.

Problematic textbook content is also a focus in this chapter, specifically, content that either (i) fails to promote social cohesion and respect for diversity or (ii) succeeds in transmitting false or skewed historical accounts. The roles of curricula (which, in theory, influence textbook content) and teacher training are also discussed because teachers deliver curricula, in part, via textbooks. If schools are to succeed in promoting social cohesion, they will need to align the supportive new curriculum (including the examination curriculum) with textbook content and teacher training.

Education: Part of the Problem, Part of the Solution

Causes of civil conflict include ethnicity, religion, entrenched poverty, social and political inequities, greed, and indignity. Young people's views of others are shaped by a range of factors including personal experiences in the home and in their communities, peer-group influence, and school experiences. Children are, first and foremost, members of families and communities from which they internalize many of their attitudes toward other groups. Research in Northern Ireland highlighted the extent to which the seeds of intolerance are planted before the child enters school. Children on both sides of the political divide there learned early on to recoil in response to symbols associated with the other side (Connolly, Smith, and Kells 2002).

Working from such foundations, formal education systems can aggravate civil unrest through curricula, textbooks, or teachers who portray minority groups or non-nationals in negative stereotypical terms (Bush and Saltarelli 2000). Governments have traditionally used educational systems to promote political and religious agendas through formal curricula and prescribed textbooks. Colonial powers employed textbooks that inculcated respect and admiration for the mother government. One Irish study demonstrates that after the early nineteenth-century political union of Ireland and Great Britain, the state education authority published readers that "contained . . . only incidental references to Ireland." The textbooks, "in effect aimed at the obliteration of all Irish traditions of culture and nationality" (Ireland 1954: 44). While something of an overstatement, this passage demonstrates the overtly political agendas of textbooks and formal education systems (Coolahan 1977). In the United States, during the nineteenth century, schoolbook authors expressed virtual unanimity "on the evil results of labor unions" (Elson 1964: 42).

Religious hatreds were also advanced. During this period the *New England Primer* advised, "Child behold the Man of Sin, the Pope, worthy of thy utmost hatred" (Luke 1991: 169).

Changing Priorities

Major shifts in forms of government and in national political priorities may have substantive repercussions within educational systems. Signal events, like national independence, tend to spark curriculum revisions and the introduction of new textbooks. In Ireland, for example, following the gaining of independence from Great Britain, there was a reaction to the non-national tone of much of the literature in school textbooks. One report of the time noted that revised textbooks "should be as far as possible emptied of specifically English thought and culture" (Educational Co. 1921). More recently, following the collapse of the Soviet Union, successor governments in the newly independent republics used textbooks to help foster new national identities. In China, too, changes in political ideology have produced revised political content in its textbooks. In the 1959 textbook series, close to a third of topics focused on revolutionary spirit and communism; in the 1993 textbook series, less than 3 percent was devoted to the same topics (Fairbrother 2003). Prompted by its bitter apartheid experiences, South Africa has made education for social cohesion a national priority and is striving to use it to foster democracy, human dignity, equality, and social justice.

Many education systems have gone too far, promoting teaching material that cultivates an overweening national pride, often based on false, or idealized, historical accounts. Many have added to the problem by making selective use of stories and history, failing to recognize the contributions of minority groups, or by misrepresenting the achievements of traditional foes.

History Books

Some of the most virulent debates focus on history books. Some see the subject of history as a vehicle that transmits ideas about patriotism to young people (Paxton 1999). State-approved books represent the national story that the government wishes to tell its young people, hoping to (i) create loyal citizens around a shared collective identity, (ii) bring about cultural integration, and (iii) encourage attitudes about an ideal community (Altbach 1991; Apple and Christian-Smith 1991; Dance 1967). These books frequently extol the "exceptional" qualities of the country and attempt to create an imagined community, a sense of group unity, and loyalty to the nation state (Wertsch 1997). Events of dubious merit—for example, massacres of indigenous peoples, land grabs, war crimes, official turpitude—tend to be excised from textbooks. Few authors appear to appreciate the professional historian's view that history is an ongoing debate, constantly refreshed by new evidence and new interpretation, and less an agreed and static set of facts or truths (Ravitch 2003).

Textbooks: Some Examples

Here we study examples from a number of countries of how textbooks have been used to promote nationalistic or religious agendas that do little to promote respect for diversity and tolerance. The evidence is categorized under eight headings: narrow nationalism, religious bias, omission, imbalance, historical inaccuracy, treatment of physical force and militarism, use of persuasive techniques, and artwork. The categories are neither exhaustive nor mutually exclusive; some material could be assigned to more than one category.

Narrow Nationalism

In this context, narrow nationalism refers to a pronounced, uncritical devotion to one's country or state. In post-Soviet Czechoslovakia, for instance, some of the textbooks that replaced the communist-era books were narrowly nationalistic and even xenophobic and racist. Some textbooks and curricula produced in the former Yugoslav nations in the 1990s (Bosnia, Croatia, Herzegovina, Montenegro, Serbia, and Slovenia), were, likewise, offensive and discriminatory to minority populations. Efforts to promote peaceful coexistence in Bosnia and Herzegovina among Bosnians, Croats, and Serbs were not helped by the country's recourse to three different curricula, each promoting a narrow national identity at the expense of the other two ethnic groups. The Office of the High Representative for Bosnia and Herzegovina (1999), created by the 1995 Dayton Peace Accord, established a panel to review textbooks and identify offensive material. The panelists, drawn from Bosnia, Croatia, and Serbia, found biased material in history textbooks in particular, but they also identified bias in books for language, literature, geography, music, culture, and art.

In the United States, textbooks have tended to present an idealized version of American history. One author describes popular social studies textbooks as "essentially nationalist histories written .. to tell children what their elders need them to know about their country" (Fitzgerald 1979). Titles portray this tendency: *The Great Experiment, The American Way, Land of the Free, Land of Promise, Triumph of the American Nation, The American Pageant*, and *The Great Republic* (Fitzgerald 1979; Loewen 1996). According to Cornbelth (2002), U.S. curricula and textbooks have striven for "celebratory" nation building and tended to present history as a national epic. Students are rarely exposed to different points of view—new national history standards released in 1994 were hotly challenged for their multiple perspectives of individual events (Cheney 1994). In the opinion of one commentator (Loewen 2000), teachers and textbooks fail to give students the tools to understand their society and in the process help foster an "unthinking nationalism" (171).

In Japan, textbook depictions of World War II remain a divisive subject (Gerow 2000; McCormack 2000; Yoshiko and Hiromitsu 2000). Prewar Japanese texts tended toward ultranationalism. Since the war, the government has been subjected to criticism over textbook content, despite the fact that most current high school textbooks contain critical analysis of Japan's conduct of the war (Hein and Selden 2000). In 2000 a new history book was written by a group of educators concerned with the lack of Japanese patriotism. Critics responded with concern that the new book represented a return to the prewar ultranationalism. China as well as North and South Korea expressed strong resentment of the Japanese government's decision to approve the new history textbook, complaining that the book failed to describe Japan's 1937 "Rape of Nanjing," and the treatment of so-called comfort women held by Japanese authorities as sex slaves. Following a detailed content analysis of the 2000 publication, South Korea asked Japan's Education Ministry to make 35 specific revisions. Japan agreed to make two. South Korea expressed displeasure by temporarily withdrawing its ambassador in 2000. The new book met with little popular demand from local Japanese school authorities, who chose instead rival textbooks. Earlier, pressure from China and Korea is credited with getting Japan to accept that its textbooks should be sensitive in their treatment of historical events involving neighboring Asian countries it conquered and occupied in wartime (Woods 2002).

In 2005, the Japanese Society for History Textbook Reform, a conservative organization, published a similar history textbook. The book was roundly criticized within Japan and used in very few schools. Nevertheless, China reacted strongly to its publication. In several cities thousands took to the streets to express their distaste for the failure of the Japanese to cover adequately the misdeeds of their troops during World War II. Several Japanese-themed shops in China were damaged. The protest expanded to include Japan's claim for a seat on the UN Security Council and other issues.

Religious Bias

Given the role religious groups and persons have long played in all aspects of education, it is not surprising to detect religious views in approved textbooks. Over the past 200 years, class or basal readers in the United States have tended to support dominant political, religious, and economic values. Children learning to read and write were also absorbing overtly religious, nationalist, racist, sexist, and vigorously procapitalist views (Kaestle 1981). In the late 1980s, an Alabama court barred the use of 44 textbooks in classrooms on the grounds that they promoted "secular humanism" (Norris 1987). The teaching in science classes of "creationism" (a Bible-based account of the origins of life, favored by evangelical Christians) versus theories of evolution is a persistent and divisive issue in the United States.

In Pakistan, General Zia-ul-Haq, during his time in power (1977–88), ardently promoted the Islamicization of Pakistani education. Following a review of the country's curriculum and textbooks in 2002, a group of Pakistani academics reported that the Islamicized curriculum and textbooks contained material they saw as insensitive to religious diversity (Nayyar and Salim 2003). Among the most serious problems, they found, were perspectives that encouraged prejudice, bigotry, and discrimination toward fellow citizens, especially women and religious minorities, and toward other nations. Textbooks also emphasized the superiority of Islam over Hinduism. Likewise, Pakistani social studies textbooks contained polemical and narrowly nationalistic and religious content.

The current curriculum for social studies for grades 1 to 5 (Pakistan 2002) places considerable emphasis on religion (Nayyar and Salim 2003). Repeated efforts by civilian governments have failed to change the emphasis on religion and nationalism in the curriculum prepared by the Ministry of Education. Elsewhere in the region, Islam is strongly promoted in Saudi textbooks. A lesson for six-year-olds notes, "all religions other than Islam are false" (Whitaker 2004).[1]

In 2000 Pakistan's immediate neighbor, India, through its National Council of Educational Research (NCERT), produced a new national curriculum. Critics have noted its Hindu bias and narrow nationalism. The Indian curriculum presents Hin-

---

[1] In an interview on CBS (Stahl 2002), the Saudi foreign minister acknowledged that approximately 15 percent of textbook material was either "abhorrent" or "questionable."

duism as the "essence" of Indian culture, casting other religions as "alien" (Bidwai 2002; *Hindustan Times* 2001). Controversy erupted after NCERT and the Central Board of Secondary Education decided to delete "objectionable paragraphs" from history texts, some of which had been in print for 25 years. The redacted passages mentioned beef-eating Hindus (a taboo practice) and described the exploitation of the lower social classes under the caste system. Professional historians and others argued that the redactions in effect censored history, promoted anti-Muslim bigotry, and perpetuated inaccurate accounts of Hindu life (Bates 2000; Sanghvi 2001). The Indian Supreme Court ruled in support of the NCERT and the Central Board of Secondary Education.

In South Africa, until the demise of apartheid, some textbooks tended to emphasize the privileged relationship that the politically dominant Afrikaners had with God (see chapter 4 in this volume). God was portrayed only in relation to the white Afrikaner. Faiths and doctrines other than the dominant group's Dutch Reformed Church (a Calvinist denomination) merited only incidental references (Du Preez 1983).

Omission

Omission is just that—the omission of text that would explain significant contributions of nondominant groups or the failure to recognize the existence of others. In some instances, omission may not be deliberate, as when there is simply too much material to cover, or when textbook writers are unaware of, or never studied, the contributions of certain national subcultures. Most history textbooks tend to take a parochial view of international events (Fitzgerald 2004; Lindaman and Ward 2004). Pakistani textbooks sometimes omit references to the Hindu and Buddhist dynasties that ruled what is now Pakistan (Hoodbhoy 2000; Nayyar and Salim 2003). Similarly, in neighboring India, one finds scant mention in textbooks of the Mogul (Muslim) dynasties. Omission also occurs when, for example, textbooks avoid mention of untoward military interventions abroad, such as the United States' role in overthrowing democratically elected governments in Chile and Nicaragua. U.S. history textbooks tend to ignore recent events in the Middle East, in sharp contrast to the treatment of this topic in European textbooks (Lindaman and Ward 2004).

The existing Palestinian curriculum presents a mixed picture. On the one hand it promotes national aspirations, opposition to occupation, and references to peace, tolerance, and respect for other cultures, while encouraging critical thinking (Israel/Palestine Centre 2003). On the other hand, the curriculum has been deemed remiss in not addressing Israel's counternarrative. In the Middle East, discussion of territorial boundaries is a highly charged issue in curricula and textbooks. This is evident in Palestinian texts. Well-publicized criticisms (Groiss 2003a; Groiss and Manor 2001; Marcus 2000) observe that Palestinian books omit mention of Israel's existence, fail to stress either tolerance or peace with Israel, and contain maps that either do not show Israel or use other names, such as "Green Line 1948 Lands."[2] One rebuttal questioned the authors' impartiality but conceded that the new Palestinian textbooks treat Israel "with a remarkable awkwardness, reticence and inconsistency" (Brown 2001). The texts in question, however, did not employ some of the

---

[2]Similar allegations have been made by CMIP against textbooks produced in other countries in the region.

most offensive phrases attributed to them. Those phrases were in fact found in Egyptian and Jordanian books published many years earlier. Israeli authorities had allowed the books to be used in Palestinian schools long before the establishment of the Palestinian Authority.

Omission in textbooks is seen, for example, in the failure to explain entrenched poverty and the consequent appeal of radical movements, notably communism. Textbooks resort to omission in failing to address the government-sanctioned atrocities committed, for example, in Argentina, Brazil, and Uruguay. Recently, the Russian government, dissatisfied with the historical accounts of Russia in its large array of textbooks, sought more uniform histories and a refocus on patriotism by delimiting textbook choice. The twentieth-century Russian textbook selected omits mention of the ethnic deportations, purges, and mass killings under Stalin (Lipman 2004). Textbooks in Brazil underreport the many citizens of African descent, focusing on the country's European descendants (Mehan and Robert 2000).

In Sri Lanka, the secessionist ethnic conflict has taken more than 60,000 lives since the mid-1970s, causing massive emigration, internal migration, and virtual economic collapse. Some Tamils living mainly in the North-East Province have sought independence after failing to obtain adequate recognition for their culture and language (Little 1994). Frustration with the Sinhala-only language policy (no longer in effect), national curricula, and textbooks contributed to Tamil alienation (Wickramasinghe and Perera 1999). An analysis of secondary textbooks produced in the Tamil language shows omissions of key aspects of Tamil economic and cultural life (Rasanayagam and Palaniappan 1999). Historical accounts are devoted largely to Sinhalese kings. Some historical events are ignored or, when treated at all, distorted. Interestingly, the national textbook authority was unaware of the specific items that caused offense to the Tamil minority and indicated that it would have readily changed most of the offending items had it been aware of them.

Recently in Texas, conservative groups exercised their rights under the state education code to scrutinize textbooks being considered for adoption (Texas Statutes 2003). The code requires that curriculum and textbooks promote democracy, patriotism, and the free-enterprise system. Nine conservative organizations recruited 250 volunteers to pore over more than 150 books for the July 2002 review (Stille 2002). Fearful of antagonizing critics—and compromising sales—educational publishers imposed censorship of their own, effectively omitting discussion of certain topics from all textbooks. Omitted topics range from controversial people to slavery, guns, junk food, and conflict with authority; religion and physical violence are also not discussed (Ravitch 2003).

Imbalance

Imbalance occurs when there is a deliberate focus on the experiences of one side or another in a conflict; de-emphasis (minimization) is another form of imbalance. For example, national textbooks developed after Croatia's secession from Yugoslavia show imbalance. Treatment of the Balkan war is discussed primarily to promote the concept of the Croatian nation-state. Relatively little attention is devoted to the counternarratives of other formerly Yugoslav peoples. Similarly, French history textbooks demonstrate imbalance in minimizing the role of Allied forces in the liberation of Paris, while lionizing the French resistance forces (Lindaman and Ward 2004). Books used in Israel's ultra-Orthodox schools demonstrate imbalance toward

Arabs (Yovel 2000). Palestinian and Saudi textbooks are said to show bias against Israel (Groiss 2003a; Groiss and Manor 2001; Marcus 2000). Yet new textbooks produced by the Palestinian Authority are said to contain fewer negative stereotypes about Jews and Israelis than those published externally (Israel/Palestine 2003). Independent reports note that although the new books are not perfect, they show no evidence of fact falsification, doctored statistics, or the promotion of hatred toward Israel (Israel/Palestine 2003; Reiss and Ihtiyar 2003).

Imbalance also arises in textbooks that slight the perspective of the historically wronged or the persecuted. Imbalance also can occur regionally, within a country. This occurs in the United States, where textbooks produced for southern and northern states show bias in their accounts of the Civil War (Zimmerman 2003). Imbalance is also evident when a favored or dominant group is seldom or ever associated with abhorrent acts, while such acts are attributed to other groups. Although it is true that readers of such textbooks are learning about the range of human behaviors, they are not learning a humbling and fundamental lesson of history—that human beings are capable of the abhorrent and the sublime.

Historical Inaccuracy

Historical inaccuracy refers to the distortion of history either because of carelessness or for ideological purposes. Some textbooks suggest that Europeans were the first to settle America and parts of Africa and Australia. Spanish and Thai textbooks have incorrectly described Korea as a Chinese colony (Voluntary Agency Network of Korea, no date). A U.S. history text identified Sinn Fein president Gerry Adams as a Protestant leader in Northern Ireland (Gendar and Feiden 2002). Social studies textbooks in both India and Pakistan have been criticized for inaccuracies and misrepresentations (Prashant 2004; Nayar and Salim 2003). Chinese textbooks (Becker 1996) have described the death by starvation of tens of millions of people as a natural disaster, and not as a consequence of Mao's Great Leap Forward Program (1958–60). Other textbooks noted that China's Tiananmen Square protests (1989) were not protests at all but demonstrations of popular support for the government's anticorruption efforts (Higgins 1997). Newly independent countries often produce textbooks that promote ideologies rather than tell a common story remembered by those who lived through the events. For instance, Kosovar Albanian and Kosova Serb accounts of the same events are quite different (Sommers and Buckland 2004).

Physical Force and Militarism

Much of the material in school history texts has been of the self-congratulatory "drum-and-trumpet variety." National heroes have been credited with godlike qualities, and the use of military or physical force often romanticized. Major wars have been depicted in terms of battles and troop movements, while relatively little attention is given to civilian loss of life or destruction of property and cultures. Colonial nations and superpowers frequently have represented themselves as liberators and bringers of civilization; economic motives are downplayed (Farr 1986). Pakistani textbooks have been criticized for their glorification of war and the use of force and for their potential to incite violence and militancy (Nayyar and Salim 2003). The current curriculum for social studies for classes 1 through 5 (Pakistan

2002) includes references to the need to "study India's evil designs against Pakistan" (Nayyar and Salim 2003: 35). Pre–World War II Japanese texts glorified militarism (Hein and Selden 2000). From 1986 to 1994, mathematics material produced for Afghanistan primary and post-primary schools and supported by the U.S. Agency for International Development was highly politicized and had militaristic overtones. The materials included problems in basic mathematics that required children to count dead Russians, Kalashnikov rifles, and hand grenades (Fritsch 2001). In addition, textbooks were written with strong political messages to support *mujahadeen* efforts to overthrow the Soviets (Ekanayake 2000). Israeli critics claim that Palestinian textbooks glorify *jihad* and praise martyrs uncritically (Groiss and Manor 2001). In general, political gains have frequently been linked to military achievements. History books have often ignored or failed to explain the policy failures that led to military interventions in the first place. According to one U.S. study, of 28 modern U.S. history textbooks analyzed, not one questioned the legitimacy of the Vietnam war (Griffin and Marciano 1979).

Persuasive Techniques

Textbooks, curricular documents, and other reading materials have used persuasive techniques to create misapprehension, fear, bias, and prejudice. In the examples below, the italicized words have been added for emphasis:

- Pakistan: "Hindus *very cunningly* succeeded in making the British believe that the Muslims were solely responsible for the [1857] rebellion" (cited in Nayyar and Salim 2003: 21).
- Germany: In accounts of the run-up to World War II, Nazi Germany is described as having *integrated* Czechoslovakia and *annexed* Austria; mainstream narratives now describe these events as invasions (Schuddekopf and others 1967).
- China: A mathematics problem from an earlier generation of textbooks gave this not-too-subtle political message (no italics required):

In the United States of America, the number of half-starved people is twice the number of unemployed, and is five million less than the number of people who live in slums. As one-half the number of slum dwellers is eleven and half-million, what is the number of unemployed in the United States? (Chi Tung-Wei 1956: 46)

Words also can be used to create strong favorable and unwarranted impressions of people, events, and nationalities (Dauzat and Dauzat 1981). Examples include:

- Name-calling. Negative words, usually adjectives, are used to give a negative impression of an idea, individual, group, or nationality: *wicked* Queen, *barbaric* clan, *treacherous* idea, *indiscriminate* act, American *imperialists*, Russian *tyrant*, Arab *terrorist*, axis of *evil*, *rogue* state.[3]

---

[3]In some cases, labels attributed to individuals have changed during the course of their lives from being highly negative ("terrorist," "subversive") to highly positive ("leader," "statesperson"). The reverse also has happened. Examples of the former include Gandhi (India), Gusmao (East Timor), Kenyatta (Kenya), and Mandela (South Africa); and of the latter, Hitler (Germany), Manuel Augusto Noriega (Panama), and Pinochet (Chile).

- Use of generalities. General terms or euphemisms may be used to discourage critical evaluation and inquiry—for example, calling a class of nuclear missiles the *Peacemaker;* or describing a militant nation as the *peace-loving people* of country X.
- Testimonials. In textbooks, this practice is used to assert that well-known leaders (such as Nelson Mandela or Winston Churchill) favored approaches or beliefs espoused in the textbook. Out-of-context quotations are used to lend authority to an asserted idea or position.
- Fear. Anecdotes may be used to frighten and convince. An example would be citing war casualties or the threat of terrorism to justify increased emphasis on national defense.
- Personification. Personification makes one person, usually a leader, synonymous with all people in the country. Examples include linking all Germans with Adolf Hitler, all Ugandans with Idi Amin, or all Iraqis with Saddam Hussein.

Biases in Artwork

While generally inserted to increase student comprehension and interest, artwork can also irritate, anger, and undermine trust. Photographs, illustrations, drawings, cartoons, and maps used to illustrate textbook content can foster bias and prejudice (Pingel 1999). Artwork can foster bias when it presents stereotypical negative images of immigrants or of citizens of rival countries. Bias is evident if a textbook consistently depicts some groups in inferior, passive roles and others in superior, active roles. Attempting to show sensitivity toward the Tamil culture in Sri Lanka by putting a separate illustration of a wedding feast in Tamil language editions, the national textbook publisher confused Tamil and Muslim ceremonial wedding dresses and so succeeded in offending both minorities.

Maps in historically conquered, colonized, de- and remarcated regions like the Middle East have great potential to offend. On the one hand, maps in some Israeli textbooks anger neighboring countries with their implied territorial claims. On the other hand, Israel does not even *appear* on maps produced by some neighboring Arab nations (Groiss 2003b). Both U.S. and Japanese history textbooks have shown reluctance to feature images that discourage distaste for war. History books in the United States, which are amply illustrated, tended to omit controversial and epic photographs (Loewen 1995), such as the famous photograph taken after the My Lai massacre. Japanese authorities requested the removal from their textbooks of material such as illustrations of an air raid, a city left in ruins by the atomic bomb, and disabled veterans (Woods 2002) because they conveyed "an excessively negative impression of war" (Yoshiko and Hiromitsu 2000: 110).

Other Reading Materials

Empirical studies (including national and international assessments of reading achievement) have highlighted the importance of supplementary reading materials to both reading achievement and reading habits (Elley 1992, 1996; Greaney 1980; Guthrie and Greaney 1991; OECD/UIS 2003). Financial allocations to purchase supplemental materials and to establish classroom and school libraries have increased over the years. Many libraries contain popular reading material such as magazines and newspapers. Although most of this material is inoffensive, some inevitably features stories that may be inimical to fostering respect and tolerance. The popular press (aided by television) has helped create false stereotypes of others. For example, popular media often have portrayed Latinos as lazy, Chinese as gamblers, Italians as crooked, Turks as barbaric, Americans as crass, British as unimaginative, Germans as dour, Norwegians as unsophisticated, Danes as disorganized, Swedes as arrogant, Jews as miserly, Arabs as savage, Scots as mean, French as degenerate, and Irish as drunken. Perhaps even more damaging for children have been the deleterious stereotypes found in adventure books, comic books, and cartoons (as well as films and videos).

It is not known to what extent supplementary reading materials contain material that might contribute to political intolerance. While one suspects that this may be slight, some books or excerpts have the potential to develop unwarranted feelings of distrust about other groups. A 1983 edition of the *Oxford Children's History* described both communities in Northern Ireland in a highly stereotypical manner (Speed and Speed 1983). It referred to Protestants' "fiddling elections" and "just hating Catholics" and claimed that "nearly every Catholic in Northern Ireland is on the side of the IRA." It also said that the 13 Catholics shot dead in a march in 1972 had "asked for it" (p. 219). This edition achieved the unusual distinction of offending both communities simultaneously. Although one brief sentence at the beginning of the article ("An officer will tell us about it") disclosed that the quotations were derived from fictional interviews, the fictional nature of the message was likely to be lost on the unsophisticated young reader.

Issues To Be Addressed

Education is a necessary but not sufficient condition for the promotion of social harmony. Students' attitudes are conditioned by many factors, especially by what they learn prior to coming to school, their school experiences, their peers, and popular culture—in the form of television, video games, and films, which tend to reinforce stereotypes, making hatred easy. Education cannot compensate for society. It cannot reach out effectively to more than 115 million young people worldwide who are not in school (UNESCO 2003). Nor is it reasonable to expect education and educational materials to be effective promoters of tolerance when many children witness the effects of social unrest and war first hand.

Education can, however, play a very important role. Within the formal education system, it will be essential to align and coordinate efforts to reform curriculum, textbooks, and pedagogical practices. Tackling one of these alone is unlikely to have much impact. For instance, curriculum changes should be reflected and reinforced in new or revised textbooks and in pre- and in-service teacher-training courses. To be successful, reform efforts also will require supportive supervisory and management styles and more participatory processes within schools.

Effecting Change

Bringing about change in curricula, textbooks, and pedagogical practices to help promote respect for diversity can be difficult. Governments may not have the political clout or courage to oppose dominant interest groups. Disaffected minorities within countries may not have a political voice. Neighboring national rivals may not be invited or, if invited, may not be willing to participate in reform efforts. During periods of strife and in postconflict countries, anger and distrust may prevent reasoned debate. The process to bring about change can be very slow and contentious. In some countries, religion, nationalism, and ethnic identities may be so intertwined as to make respect for other groups a very daunting task.

History

History textbooks are particularly problematic. Educational authorities, especially in newly emerging states, frequently use curricula to promote national aspirations, which can run counter to minority aspirations and, in some instances, majority aspirations. Textbooks sometimes deliberately and systematically exclude counternarratives, especially those of minorities or a defeated people. Opposing or rival interpretations of historical events are inevitable in any country. Agreement may have to be reached on which politically unpleasant historical facts have to addressed or ignored. Finally, it will not be possible to cover all the aspects of the new national narrative/history that advocates may wish to include.

Some educational authorities view national history as a narrative of triumphs, tragedies, heroes, and villains. Those who advocate that history should be taught as a process—as opposed to a set of facts that must be memorized—suggest that young people must consider different viewpoints to gain a well-informed understanding of their country's past (Pingel 1999). While the multiple-perspective approach is likely to develop an appreciation of the "other's" situation and to foster a healthy skepticism about bygone events and personalities, some educators caution that young children may consider the approach boring. Conditioned by the modern media, they probably would prefer adventure narratives featuring brave combatants and happy endings, with their heroes emerging victorious.

Action-oriented history narratives tend to omit or slight the role of diplomacy. Many Europeans, for instance, know the names of World War II leaders such as Churchill, Hitler, and Mussolini but not those of Robert Schuman or Jean Monnet. These visionary Frenchmen promoted the idea of uniting the economic interests of democratic European nations, believing that the most important result would be the prevention of future wars among European nations.

Curriculum Reform

Curricular reform should precede textbook reform. The challenges facing curriculum personnel are both technical and political. A ministry of education wishing to use the curriculum as the agent of change should therefore consider convening representatives from key regional, ethnic, and religious groups, including some who may have been hostile toward each other and toward the government. Education ministries might be well advised to invite major interest groups to name their own candidates; this process is likely to produce more broadly acceptable candidates than if government were to name those it preferred.

Getting agreement on curricular content and values may not be easy. In the interest of promoting respect for diversity, some policymakers may choose to ignore recent sensitive historical events. Following the demise of the apartheid system of education, South Africa held a national conference on values education and democracy to help create consensus on the curriculum. It invited input from various states. Since apartheid was dismantled in 1994, stakeholder participation has become a feature of policymaking in South Africa (Republic of South Africa 2001).

Training Writers

Textbook writers and editors may benefit greatly from training in these issues. Like most people, textbook writers may be unaware of the extent of their own biases and prejudices. Such training might stress the removal of pernicious stereotypes; accurate and authentic portrayal of events, groups, and individuals; tolerance; religious sensitivity; responsible citizenry; social, civic, and moral responsibility; global awareness; balanced presentations of issues; and accurate use of illustrations. Some thought might also be given to the extent to which historical narratives (i) glorify the use of physical force and military might and (ii) minimize the effects of armed conflict on individuals, economies, and nations. Training might also focus on how to give more attention to political and diplomatic efforts to address intra- and international conflict.

In-Service Teacher Training

Teachers tend to rely on textbooks for subject-matter content. But their methods of delivering the curriculum and interpreting content can play a major role in helping students form attitudes about others. Many teachers, not having experience or appreciation of other cultures, are quite unaware of the extent of the ethnocentrism that they transmit to their pupils (Farr 1986). Teachers should be encouraged to help children read critically and to identify the writer's mood, tone, and purpose. Teachers also can promote critical thinking by observing that the same event can have alternative interpretations. This can help promote a healthy skepticism about reports of past events and interpretations. Teachers also can help the young reader adopt the perspective of the "other" as a way of feeling the injustice sometimes experienced by different parties in times of conflict. Schools might also wish to encourage greater teacher and student participation in decisionmaking on basic school-management issues.

Formal Assessment

Success in bringing about pedagogical change will require understanding and support from school inspectors and others who supervise teacher performance. Given the considerable evidence that classroom and external student assessment systems greatly influence teacher and student behavior and study habits (Kellaghan and Greaney 2001, 2004), it also will require changes in the content of high-stakes public examinations. Care should be taken to ensure that teachers' routine assessment practices (including classroom questions) and public examination questions lessen the emphasis on rote memorization and devote increased attention to higher-order cognitive skills.

Overediting

Ardent advocates of eliminating perceived biases may diminish the educational value and the literary content of some reading materials. For instance, in the interest of promoting sales, U.S. publishers have tended to steer clear of content that might give offense to any of the many existing pressure groups. Modern U.S. textbooks have been criticized for their blandness and their avoidance of controversial issues (Ravitch 2003). To help achieve a perception of impartiality, major publishers have compiled extensive lists of words, stereotypes, and topics to avoid (Ravitch 2003). Ravitch's list of close to 400 banned words includes *maid, school boy*, and *working man* (sexist); *oriental, lame,* and *insane* (offensive); *huts* (ethnocentric); *Middle East* (Eurocentric); *yacht* and *polo* (elitist), as well as *niggardly, idiot, fat*, and *devil.* Test-development companies use similar lists.

Developing Countries

The challenge of introducing pedagogical styles that promote critical thinking and respect for diversity is likely to be greatest in developing countries, in which children frequently lack access to textbooks and trained teachers (Greaney 1996). Some systems use out-of-date books,[4] and many developing countries—including China, India, and many in Africa—employ very large numbers of untrained teachers. Linguistically diverse nations (India, for example, has more than 200 languages and 10 writing systems) face additional difficulties in training teachers and in providing supportive reading material. Finally, the dominance in developing countries of the "high stakes" end-of-cycle public examination system, with its emphasis on recall, suggests that promoting critical thinking skills will be difficult.

Donors

Education reforms, especially those related to curricular reform, are generally the responsibility of the national educational authority. Bilateral and multilateral donors have contributed, and will continue to contribute, to improve curricula and textbooks in developing countries.[5] The World Bank has developed draft guidelines for staff preparing or supervising educational projects in developing countries (see James Socknat's chapter in this volume). These guidelines suggest strategies for fostering respect for diversity through interventions in teaching, curriculum, and pedagogical practices. The guidelines suggest, among other things, broad stakeholder participation in curriculum development, awareness-raising among publishers, and teacher-education courses on the importance of local traditions.

Donors might consider refusing to fund the publication of textbooks that contain divisive and inappropriate content. In some instances, however, such an approach runs the risk of being counterproductive. Governments may resent intervention in a key area of national interest such as the education curriculum. Because few international donors are able to undertake nation-specific curriculum

---

[4]In 1994 books in use in Palestinian classrooms featured pre-1967 textbooks that extolled the greatness of the Egyptian kingdom and its 20 million inhabitants. Egypt became a republic in 1953 and has a population of 65 million (Le Monde Diplomatique 2001).

[5]To date, the World Bank has funded in excess of US$2.8 billion for textbook production.

or textbook development, donors might encourage education ministries to involve key minority groups in the curriculum and textbook review process. Timely input of this nature makes sound political and educational sense. Donors might also encourage comprehensive reviews of existing textbooks and support reviews of textbook material (especially history books) in neighboring countries. Professional historians from India and in Pakistan, for example, could be convened to review their countries' standard textbooks for inaccuracy or bias. Professional historians should be included in review teams. Finally, donors could fund the training of staff members and professionals working on curriculum and textbooks; such training would focus on bias detection and effective ways to promote cohesive and peaceful societies.[6]

Broader Perspectives

Although nationalistic forces will continue to determine much of what students study, future curricula are likely to include more regional and global perspectives. This general trend is assured by the globalization of media and communication, free trade, international sporting events, and phenomena that do not respect national boundaries: international terrorism, global warming, and disease epidemics like severe acute respiratory syndrome and HIV/AIDS (Greenspan and Shanker 2002, 2003). Future curricula are likely to stress the interdependence of peoples, a development that should lead to greater awareness, understanding, and respect for differences and a greater willingness to promote peaceful, political solutions to international disputes.

Building trust can take time. After World War II, West Germany and Poland spent 15 years before agreeing on criteria and arrangements for a mutual textbook-review process. It is worth noting in this regard that British Minister Margaret Thatcher informed a former German ambassador in 1990 that it would be "at least another 40 years before the British could trust the Germans again" (Young 1999: 359).

Positive Initiatives

Many countries may have to confront difficult historical facts in drafting textbook content. In this regard, Germany appears to have been more proactive than either Japan or the United States, notably in addressing its culpability for World War II. A number of German states encourage the concept of civic responsibility to help ensure that movements such as Nazism do not recur. In many German states, the curriculum is outward looking and reflects a strong European dimension (Soysal 2000). German textbooks tend to deal frankly with the past, including the Holocaust.

A number of interesting initiatives have resulted in the withdrawal of inaccurate and harmful materials from textbooks. In France, authorities withdrew 26 books that glorified war and taught hatred for the enemy (Schuddekopf and others 1967). Starting in 1954, France and Germany established a joint textbook review process staffed by professionals. Similarly, the Czech Republic and Germany have held

---

[6]The literature on gender bias (for example, Sifuniso and others 2000) contains useful training models that might profitably be adapted for this purpose. Formal training programs are offered by institutions such as the Georg Eckert Institute in Germany and the University of Ulster in Northern Ireland.

joint review meetings, as have Bosnia, Croatia, and Serbia in the wake of the Balkan wars of the 1990s.

Sri Lanka recently introduced an innovative manuscript-review scheme requiring all new books to be vetted for sensitivity to minority interests. The government promised that it would fund the costs of producing and distributing textbooks that were judged to be sensitive to minority interests. Manuscripts that failed to meet a minimum score on the sensitivity criterion would not qualify for government funding.[7]

* * * *

Education can and has contributed to alienation, distrust, and strife. Left unexamined and unchallenged, textbooks, curricula, and teacher training can lead to jingoistic thinking and uncritical acceptance of deleterious ideologies and propaganda. However, education also can be part of the solution. Revisions of curricula, textbooks, and teaching approaches are essential early steps in developing tolerance, respect for others, and, ultimately, peace.

References

Altbach, P. G. 1991. "Textbooks: The International Dimension." In *The Politics of the Textbook,* ed. M. W. Apple and L. K. Christian-Smith, 242–58. London: Routledge.

Apple, M. W., and L. K. Christian-Smith, eds. 1991. *The Politics of the Textbook.* London: Routledge.

Bates, S. 2000. "Anger at Growing Textbook Bias in India." *The Guardian*, January 25. http://www.guardian.co.uk/.

Becker, J. 1996. *Hungry Ghosts*. New York: Free Press.

Bellamy, C. 2001. "Building a World Fit for Children." *Global Future* (3rd quarter): 1–3.

Bidwai, P. 2002. "Row Brewing on Pro-Hindu Slant in Textbooks: Major Conflict in India on Education." *South Asia Tribune,* September 23–29. http://www.satribune.com/archives/sep23_29_02/opinion_bidwai.htm.

Brown, N. J. 2001. "Democracy, History, and the Contest over the Palestinian Curriculum." Paper presented at the Adam Institute for Democracy and Peace, Jerusalem, November. http://www.geocities.com/nathanbrown1/details_cmip.html.

Bush, K. D., and D. Saltarelli. 2000. *The Two Faces of Education in Ethnic Conflict.* Florence: United Nations Children's Fund, Innocenti Centre.

Cheney, L. V. 1994. "The End of History." *Wall Street Journal*, October 26.

Chi Tung-Wei. 1956. *Education for the Proletariat in Communist China.* Hong Kong: Union Research Institute. Cited in *Socialist Mathematics Education*, ed. F. J. Swetz. Southampton, PA: Burgundy Press, 1978.

---

[7]Implementation of this program has been slow because of a number of government changes.

Colletta, N. J. 2002. "Human Security and Poverty: Implications for IFI Reform." Background paper prepared for the Global Commission on Human Security. United Nations, New York. October 22.

Connolly, P., A. Smith, and B. Kells. 2002. *Too Young to Notice? The Cultural and Political Awareness of 3–6 Year Olds in Northern Ireland.* Belfast: Community Relations Council.

Coolahan, J. 1977. Three Eras of English Reading in Irish National Schools. In *Studies in Reading,* ed. V. Greaney, 12–26. Dublin: Educational Co.

Cornbleth, C. 2002. Images of America: What Youth DO Know about the United States. *American Educational Research Journal* 39 (2): 519–52.

Dance, E. H. 1967. "Bias in History Teaching and Textbooks." In *History Teaching and History Textbook Revision.* Strasbourg: Council for Cultural Co-operation of the Council of Europe.

Dauzat, J. A., and S. V. Dauzat. 1981. *Reading: The Teacher and the Learner.* New York: Wiley.

Du Preez, J. M. 1983. *Africana Afrikaner: Meestersimbole in Suid-Afrikaanse Skoolhandboeke.* Alberton: Librarius Felicitas.

Educational Company. 1921. Draft report of National Programme Conferences. Dublin.

Ekanayake, S. B. 2000. *Education in the Doldrums: Afghan Tragedy.* Islamabad: Al-Noor.

Elley, W. B. 1992. *How in the World do Students Read?* Hamburg: International Association for the Evaluation of Educational Achievement.

———. 1996. "Using Book Floods to Raise Literacy Levels." In *Promoting Reading in Developing Countries,* ed. V. Greaney, 148–62. Newark, DE: International Reading Association.

Elson, R. M. 1964. *Guardians of Tradition: American Schoolbooks in the Nineteenth Century.* Lincoln: University of Nebraska Press.

Epstein, T. 1997. "Sociocultural Approaches to Young People's Historical Understanding." *Social Education* 61 (1): 28–31.

Fairbrother, G. P. 2003. *Toward Critical Patriotism: Student Resistance to Political Education in Hong Kong and China.* Hong Kong: Hong Kong University Press.

Farr, R. 1986. "Social Worlds of Childhood." In *Children: Needs and Rights,* ed. V. Greaney, 21–42. New York: Irvington.

FitzGerald, F. 1979. *America Revised: History Schoolbooks in the Twentieth Century.* New York: Vintage Books.

———. 2004. "The View from Out There." Review of *History Lessons: How Textbooks from around the World Portray U.S. History,* by D. Lindaman and K. Ward. *Washington Post,* August 8, T01.

Fritsch, P. 2001. "With Pakistan's Schools in Tatters, *Madrasahs* Spawn Young Warriors." *Wall Street Journal,* October 2.

Gendar, A., and D. Feiden. 2002. Schoolbooks are Flubbing Facts: Texts Filled with Errors and Political Correctness. *New York Daily News,* December 21.

Gerow, A. 2000. Consuming Asia, Consuming Japan. In *Censoring History: Citizenship and Memory in Japan, Germany, and the United States*, ed. L. Hein and M. Selden, 74–95. Armonk, NY: M. E. Sharpe.

Greaney, V. 1980. "Factors Related to Amount and Type of Leisure Reading." *Reading Research Quarterly* 25: 337–57.

———. 1996. "Reading in Developing Countries: Problems and Issues." In *Promoting Reading in Developing Countries*, ed. V. Greaney, 5–38. Newark, DE: International Reading Association.

———. 1996. *Promoting Reading in Developing Countries*. Newark, DE: International Reading Association.

Greenspan, S. I., and S. G. Shanker. 2002. *Toward a Psychology of Global Interdependence: A Framework for International Cooperation*. Bethesda, MD: Council on Human Development.

———. 2003. "Why an International Family and Children's Policy Is Essential for Spreading Democracy in an Interdependent World." Unpublished manuscript.

Griffin, W., and J. Marciano. 1979. "Teaching the Vietnam War." Montclair, N.J.: Allanheld, Osmun. Cited in *Censoring History: Citizenship and Memory in Japan, Germany and the United States*, ed. L Hein and M. Selden, 163. Armonk, NY: M. E. Sharpe.

Groiss, A. 2003a. "Jews, Israel, and Peace in Palestinian Textbooks: The New Textbooks for Grades 3 and 8." Center for Monitoring the Impact of Peace, New York and Jerusalem.

———. 2003b. "The West, Christians, and Jews in Saudi Arabian Schoolbooks." Center for Monitoring the Impact of Peace, New York and Jerusalem.

Groiss, A., and Y. Manor, eds. 2001. "Jews, Israel, and Peace in Palestinian Textbooks, 2000–2001 and 2001–2002." Center for Monitoring the Impact of Peace, New York and Jerusalem.

Guthrie, J. T., and V. Greaney. 1991. "Literacy Acts." In *Handbook of Reading Research,* ed. R. Barr, M. L. Kamil, P. Mosenthal, and P. D. Pearson, 68–96. New York: Macmillan.

Hanushek, E. A. 1995. "Interpreting Recent Research on Schooling in Developing Countries." *World Bank Research Observer* 10: 227–46.

Hamburg, D. A. 1984. "Prejudice, Ethnocentrism, and Violence in an Age of High Technology." *Carnegie Corporation of New York Annual Report*. New York.

Hein, L., and M. Selden, eds. 2000. *Censoring History: Citizenship and Memory in Japan, Germany, and the United States*. Armonk, NY: M. E. Sharpe.

Heyneman, S. P., and W. Loxley. 1983. "The Effect of Primary School Quality on Achievement across Twenty-Nine High- and Low-Income Countries." *American Journal of Sociology* 88: 1162–94.

Higgins, A. 1997. "Patriotic Pens Rewrite History." *The Guardian*, October 13, 17.

Hindustan Times. 2001. "How the HRD Ministry Went About Its Task of Saffronisation." *Hindustan Times* (Lucknow), November 25.

Hoodbhoy, P. 2000. "What Are They Teaching in Pakistani Schools Today?" *Particle Politics.* Online at http://www.chowk.com.

Ireland Department of Education. 1954. *Report of the Council of Education.* Dublin: Stationery Office.

Israel/Palestine Center for Research and Information. 2003. "Analysis and Evaluation of the New Palestinian Curriculum." Report submitted to the Public Affairs Office, U.S. Consulate General, Jerusalem. March.

Kaestle, C. F. 1981. "Literacy and Mainstream Culture in American History." *Language Arts* 58.

Kellaghan, T., and V. Greaney. 2001. *Using Assessment to Improve the Quality of Education.* Paris: UNECSO IIEP.

Le Monde Diplomatique. 2001. A Textbook Case: Israel or Palestine. Who Teaches What History? http://mondeldiplo.com/2001/07/11textbook.

Lindaman, D., and K. Ward. 2004. *History Lessons: How Textbooks from around the World Portray U.S. History.* New York: New Press.

Lipman, M. 2004. Rewriting History for Putin. *Washington Post,* March 21, B7.

Little, D. 1994. *Sri Lanka: The Invention of Enmity.* Washington, DC: United States Institute of Peace.

Loewen, J. W. 1996. *Lies My Teacher Told Me: Everything Your American History Textbook Got Wrong.* New York: New Press.

———. 2000. "The Vietnam War in High School American History." In *Censoring History: Citizenship and Memory in Japan, Germany, and the United States,* ed. L. Hein and M. Selden, 150–72. Armonk, NY: M. E. Sharpe.

Luke, A. 1991. "The Secular Word: Catholic Reconstruction of Dick and Jane." In *The Politics of the Textbook,* ed. M. W. Apple and L. K. Christian-Smith, 166–90. London: Routledge.

Lundberg, I., and P. Linnakyla. 1992. *Teaching Reading around the World.* Hamburg: International Association for the Evaluation of Educational Achievement.

Machel, G. 2000. "The Impact of Armed Conflict on Children. A Critical Review of Progress Made and Obstacles Encountered in Increasing Protection for War-Affected Children." Available from www.waraffectedchildren.com/machel–e.asp. Accessed May 2005.

Marcus, I. 2000. *Palestinian Authority Teachers' Guides.* New York and Jerusalem: Center for Monitoring the Impact of Peace.

Matsuura, K., J. Wolfensohn, T. Obaid, C. Bellamy, and M. Malloch Brown. 2001. "Harness the Power of Education." UNESCO Statement 2001–65. Paris. April 27.

McCormack, G. 2000. "The Japanese Movement to Correct History." In *Censoring History: Citizenship and Memory in Japan, Germany, and the United States,* ed. L. Hein and M. Selden, 53–73. Armonk, NY: M. E. Sharpe.

Mehan, H. B., and S. A. Robert. 2000. "Thinking the Nation: Textbook Representations and Regions in Asia and Latin America." CILAS Working Paper 19. San Diego: University of California at San Diego.

Mills, G. 2002. *Poverty to Prosperity: Globalisation, Good Governance, and African Recovery.* Capetown: South African Institute of International Affairs and Tafelberg Publishers.

Mungoven, R. 2001. "Children: A Forbidden Weapon of War." *Global Future* (3rd quarter): 9–10.

Nayyar, A. H., and A. Salim. 2003. "Project on Civil Society Initiatives in Curricula and Textbook Reform." Islamabad: Sustainable Development Policy Institute. www.sdpi.org.

Norris, B. 1987. "Creationists Lose Battle but Keep Faith." *Times Educational Supplement,* March 7, 12.

OECD/UNESCO Institute of Statistics. 2003. *Literacy Skills for the World of Tomorrow—Further Results from PISA 2000.* Paris and Montreal.

Office of the High Representative. 1999. "Overview of Educational Problems in BiH and Guidelines for Intervention." Sarajevo. September 1. Available from www.ohr.int/print/?content_id=5121. Accessed May 2005.

Pakistan Ministry of Education. 2002. *National Curriculum. Social Studies for Classes 1–V.* Islamabad. Cited in "Project on Civil Society Initiatives in Curricula and Textbook Reform," by A. H. Nayyar and A. Salim, 35. Islamabad: Sustainable Development Policy Institute, 2003.

Paxton, R. J. 1999. "A Deafening Silence: History Textbooks and the Students Who Read Them." *Review of Educational Research* 69: 315–39.

Pingel, F. 1999. *UNESCO Guidebook on Textbook Research and Textbook Revision.* Paris. UNESCO.

Prashant, S. J. 2004. Withdraw Immediately Standard VIII Social Science Textbook. Centre for Human Rights, Justice, and Peace, Navrangpura, Ahmedabad, Gujarat, India. Available from http://bocs.hu/india/prashant-withdraw-textbook.htm. Accessed May 2005.

Rasanayagam, Y., and V. Palaniappan. 1999. "Education and Social Cohesion Analysis of Potential Ethno-Cultural and Religious Bias in the School Textbooks of History and Social Studies for Years 7, 8, 10, and 11." University of Colombo, Sri Lanka. Unpublished paper.

Ravitch, D. 2003. *The Language Police.* New York: Knopf.

Reiss, W., and N. Ihtiyar. 2003. "An Analysis of Selected Natural Science and Mathematics Textbooks." Georg Eckert Institute for International Textbook Research, Braunschweig, Germany.

Romsics, I. 1999. *Hungary in the Twentieth Century.* Budapest: Corvina.

Sanghvi, V. 2001. "Talibanising Our Education." *Hindustan Times* (Lucknow), November 25.

Schuddekopf, O., E. Bruley, E. H. Dance, and H. Vigander. 1967. *History Teaching and History Textbook Revision.* Strasbourg: Council for Cultural Co-operation of the Council of Europe.

Seixas, P. 1993. "Historical Understanding among Adolescents in a Multicultural Setting." *Curriculum Inquiry* 23: 301–27.

Sifuniso, M., C. Kasonde, E.N. Kimani, I. Maimbolwa-Sinyangwe, W. Kimani, and M. Nalumango. 2000. "Gender-Sensitive Editing." Working Group on Books and Learning Materials, Association for the Development of Education in Africa, Education Department, Department for International Development, London.

Sommers, M., and P. Buckland. 2004. *Parallel Worlds: Rebuilding the Education System in Kosovo. A Case Study.* Paris: UNESCO, International Institute for Educational Planning.

South Africa. 2001. *Education in South Africa: Achievements since 1994.* Pretoria: Department of Education.

Soysal, Y. N. 2000. "Identity and Transnationalization in German School Textbooks." In *Censoring History: Citizenship and Memory in Japan, Germany, and the United States,* ed. L. Hein and M. Selden, 127–49. Armonk, NY: M. E. Sharpe.

Speed, P., and M. Speed. 1983. *The Oxford Children's History 2: The Making of the Modern Age.* Oxford: Oxford University Press.

Stahl, L. 2002. Interview with Saudi Arabian Foreign Minister Prince Sa'ud al-Faysal. CBS "60 Minutes," September 9.

Stille, A. 2002. "Textbook Publishers Learn to Avoid Messing with Texas." *New York Times,* June 29.

Texas. 2003. Texas Statutes: Education Code. Available at http://www.capitol.state.tx.us/statutes/edtoc.html. Accessed May 2005.

UNESCO. 2003. *EFA Global Monitoring Report 2003/4. Gender and Education for All: The Leap to Equality.* Paris.

UNICEF. 1996. *Impact of Armed Conflict on Children. The Report of Graca Machel.* New York.

United Kingdom. 2000. *Eliminating World Poverty: Making Globalization Work for the Poor.* Government White Paper. London: Her Majesty's Stationery Office.

United Nations. 1948. "Universal Declaration of Human Rights." General Assembly Resolution 44/25, November 20. New York: United Nations.

———. 1989. "Convention of the Rights of the Child." General Assembly Resolution 217 A (III), December 10. New York.

Voluntary Agency Network of Korea. No date. "Textbook Improvement to Enhancing Mutual Understanding." Available from http://www.prkorea.com/english/textbook.html. Accessed May 2005.

Watchlist on Children and Armed Conflict. 2002. "The Impact of Conflict on Children in Occupied Palestinian Territory and Israel. New York." September 13.

Wertsch, J. V. 1997. Narrative Tools of History and Identity. *Culture and Psychology* 3: 5–20.

Whitaker, B. 2004. "Saudi Textbooks 'Demonise' West." *Guardian Unlimited*, July 14. www.guardian.co.uk/saudi/story/0,11599, 1260867,00.html.

Wickramasinghe, N., and S. Perera. 1999. "Assessment of Ethno-Cultural and Religious Bias in Social Studies and History Texts of Years 7, 8, 10, and 11." University of Colombo, Sri Lanka. Unpublished paper.

Woods, K. 2002. History Textbook Controversies in Japan. ERIC Digest, ED464010. http://www.ericfacility.net/databases/ERIC_Digests/index/index.cfm.

Yoshiko, N., and I. Hiromitsu. 2000. "Japanese Education, Nationalism, and Ienega Saburo's Textbook Lawsuits." In *Censoring History: Citizenship and Memory in Japan, Germany and the United States*, ed. L. Hein and M. Selden, 96–126. Armonk, NY: M. E. Sharpe.

Young, H. 1999. *This Blessed Plot: Britain and Europe from Churchill to Blair.* Woodstock, NY: Overlook Press.

Yovel, A. 2000. "Arabs and Palestinians in Israeli Textbooks in the School Year 1999–2000." Center for Monitoring the Impact of Peace, New York and Jerusalem.

Zimmerman, J. 2003. "Iraq's Textbooks—and Ours." *Washington Post*, July 13, B07.

4

Textbooks in South Africa from Apartheid to Post-Apartheid: Ideological Change Revealed by Racial Stereotyping

Alta Engelbrecht

After 1948, as a result of the ideology of apartheid, curricula in South African schools became entrenched in prejudice, stigmatization, and stereotyping (Van de Rheede 1992; Strydom 1997). As an ideology of superiority, the purpose of apartheid was to secure power to allow the dominant Afrikaner values—white and Western—to prevail. To retain power, the dominant group discriminated against, humiliated, and violently oppressed less powerful groups. The opinions and ideas of these oppressed groups were marginalized by the dominant group to the extent that the former had no voice and may as well have been invisible (Department of Systematic Theology 2000).

What role did the ideology of apartheid play in the organized knowledge system of South African society? By their nature, textbooks tend to control knowledge as well as transmit it, and reinforce selected cultural values in learners. They act as an officially sanctioned version of knowledge and culture and, consequently, have the power to foster judgmental perspectives (Marsden 2001). During the apartheid era, only positive aspects of the Afrikaners' past were portrayed in South African textbooks (Chernis 1990; Du Plessis and Du Plessis 1987; Strydom 1997). Differences between whites and nonwhites were highlighted to establish a more favorable disposition for the white in-group and to justify the actions of this group (Webb 1992; Spencer 1997; Van der Merwe 2000). People of color were, through simplification and overgeneralization, reduced to a few simple, essential characteristics or stereotypes (Esterhuyse 1986; Du Preez 1983).

In 1983 a significant study by J. M. Du Preez, analyzing 53 textbooks used in black and white Afrikaans and English schools, had a huge impact on the South African textbook landscape. One of the outcomes of the study was the identification of Afrikaner master symbols that lay at the core of the Afrikaner identity during the apartheid era. The 12 master symbols identified in the Du Preez study are:

- Whites are superior, while blacks are inferior.
- Legal authority is not questioned.
- The Afrikaner has a privileged relationship with God.
- South Africa rightfully belongs to the Afrikaner.
- The Afrikaner is a Boer nation.[1]
- South Africa and the Afrikaner are isolated.

---

[1]Boer here means a farmer, thus suggesting "a nation of farmers."

- The Afrikaner is militarily innovative and resourceful.
- The Afrikaner has always felt threatened.
- World opinion of South Africa is important.
- South Africa is a leader in Africa.
- The Afrikaner has a God-given task to fulfill in Africa.
- South Africa is an afflicted country.

Master symbols in textbooks determine the sociocultural generalizations of a society to the extent that they become part of society's collective consciousness, that is, deep-rooted perspectives according to which the world is interpreted. They form the lens through which everything is seen, experienced, and evaluated (Du Preez 1983; Polakow-Suransky 2002; Chernis 1990). The scars of these master symbols in the official curriculum, as well as the hidden and null[2] curricula, were deep and firmly in place in the South African education system for 40 years. During this time, the school and the textbook acted as a "reproductive force in an unequal society" (Apple 1990: 31).

Many researchers believe that textbooks in history, geography, language, and religious instruction, in particular, reflect the social construction of knowledge in a society (Marsden 2001; Higgs 1995; Webb 1992). Several studies have shown how for decades South African textbooks were entrenched with racism, sexism, stereotypes, and historical inaccuracies (Auerbach 1965; Siebörger 1992; Esterhuyse 1986; Du Preez 1983; Bundy 1993). The emphasis in this chapter will be on textbooks used in history and Afrikaans courses. Both are of great importance in the construction of identity. Through their narratives both raise sensitive issues about the apartheid legacy institutionalized by the "white Afrikaners."[3]

History Textbooks

The issue of history textbooks has been at the center of the educational reform debate in South Africa for over a decade. University of Pretoria historian Charles van Onselen considers the textbook debate "a playground for ideologues and politicians" (Polakow-Suransky 2002: 3), because, as Apple and Christian-Smith explain:

> Textbooks embody the *selective tradition*—it is always someone's selection, someone's vision of legitimate knowledge and culture, one that in the process of enfranchising one group's cultural capital disenfranchises another's (1991: 4).

Under apartheid, history was offered in a way that justified Afrikaner domination and Afrikaner struggles for self-determination. That heroic struggle for survival formed the core of the South African history curriculum.

Peter Kallaway, history professor at the University of the Western Cape, believes that, in retrospect, apartheid history was not so much deliberate distortion as a tak-

---

[2]Null curricula are the options that learners are not offered, which thus will not be part of their repertoire.

[3]This term is enclosed in quotations to indicate that the author is aware that "white Afrikaners" are ideologically diverse, and because the term refers to Afrikaners, to whom whiteness was a proviso for their core identity.

ing for granted of a particular perspective that was then enforced (History Education Group 1993).

History is never a static set of facts; it is always a dynamic process of understanding. In his study of South African history syllabi and textbooks between 1839 and 1990, Chernis notes that, through the use of master symbols, texts create an implicit "other":

> A nation's self-image, portrayed as flatteringly as possible in its history textbooks, is to a large extent defined by the manner in which it views others. It is almost as if the self-image is enhanced by the co-existence of hostile images of those deemed outside the group (1990: 59).

In the past, the threat to Afrikanerdom lay in everything that was non-Afrikaans. The chief threats included the English, urbanization, both foreign and other African states, the future, communism, and, in particular, the large black South African population. Staunching the danger by attributing negative symbols to these threats, especially out-groups, trapped the Afrikaner in a vicious circle.

Threat is the wellspring of the phenomenon whereby people who reject one out-group are inclined to reject other out-groups, with the implication that being anti-something can culminate in being anti-everything. Prejudice and the perception of danger and threat then were reinforced by segregation, the institutionalized form of discrimination (Du Preez 1983).

History for Standard 6–10 (Joubert and Britz 1975) was a popular series in both English and Afrikaans schools during the apartheid era. Polakow-Suransky (2002) describes numerous examples in which that work glorified and legitimized "white settlement." The book explained the apartheid policy of separate development as follows:

> If all the different population groups of South Africa were included in one system, one or more groups would inevitably dominate the others. . . . The established nationhood of the whites has to be protected and maintained in that part of the country that has *always* been theirs (Joubert and Britz 1975: 247, emphasis added).

This quotation reveals at least two master symbols: *the Afrikaner has always felt threatened* and therefore has to be protected from "the others"; and *South Africa rightfully belongs to the Afrikaner.*

Another fundamental master symbol relevant here is that *the Afrikaner has a privileged relationship with God.* This belief implies that the Supreme Being ordained that there should be an eternal divide between white and black. The highest value in the apartheid symbology is the preservation of a dominant white culture, which invokes another master symbol: *whites are superior, while blacks are inferior.*

Chernis (1990: 338) characterizes the Joubert series as "anti-knowledge" because of the legitimizing of the Afrikaner political system and nationalist mythology. A more recent textbook, *Making History, Grade 12* (Pape and others 1998), contradicts Joubert's rhetoric of separate development. Yet another new book, *Looking into the Past, Grade 10* (Seleti and others 1999) points to an even greater shift toward reversing the apartheid doctrine:

> [The Group Areas Act] which broke up entire communities and led to large scale forced removals . . . further restricted the mobility of Africans and led

to many cases of extreme hardship. Bantu education impoverished genera-tions of African children. The total impact was sufficient for the international community to call apartheid a crime against humanity (317).

This shift was the start of the critical engagement of history with issues, an engagement Bam calls "highlighting the contradictions of a given society" (2000: 4). But first clarity was necessary as to what type of school history would surface in a post-apartheid curriculum. There were two options in particular. Should apartheid history be countered with African nationalist views and narratives (an approach called history from below or people's history)? Or should a synthesized account of the past be the objective?

Three problems complicated these questions. First, the new curriculum, known as Curriculum 2005, placed history in a broader category of social sciences and geog-raphy, one that called for the mastery of basic geography and historical facts. As a result, a content-driven approach was downplayed significantly, diluting the sub-ject. Critical analysis of the multilayered South African narratives had to be ignored. Although South African society went through a dramatic public truth and reconcili-ation ritual, debriefing of the past through history instruction was not to be.

Second, the new government, and specifically former minister of education Sibusiso Bengu, were criticized in the first years of democracy for the continued use of discredited history textbooks from the apartheid era—especially in the most impoverished classrooms in South Africa. The government, and specifically Minis-ter Bengu, delayed the implementation of the new curriculum. The delay was blamed on a lack of funding, but some critics attributed it to an effort to diffuse ten-sion. Only after a new education minister, Kader Asmal, had been appointed was a history/archaeology panel established to analyze the quality of history teaching and to strengthen the history curriculum. The panel insisted that "promoting strong study of the past is a particular educational imperative in a country like South Africa" and that government policy, consciously or unconsciously, had deemphasized history in schools and in tertiary sectors (Polakow-Suransky 2002).

Third, especially in traditionally white schools, the Afrikaner nationalist narra-tive has not died easily. Since 1994, white South Africans have become increasingly apolitical, and this trend has resulted in the historical ignorance of young whites. Very few new history texts are written in Afrikaans, emphasizing the withdrawal and neutrality of white Afrikaners who, ironically, had institutionalized apartheid. At the same time, the contentiousness of political issues makes it very difficult to teach about the apartheid period. Parents complain about political issues being raised in history classes. In response, teachers have tended to move away from text-books—old and new—and increasingly rely on providing students with their own material, such as newspaper articles or photocopied selections from different text-books.

It was only recently, at the Ten-Year Celebration of Freedom in Cape Town on March 31, 2004, that Education Minister Asmal announced several new resources for teaching and learning about history, produced under the auspices of the South African History Project. Some of these resources are for teachers only and include reference works and teaching materials. Now there is something for everyone: from primary and secondary school teachers to researchers. Some of these resources are:

- A new book for high school students and teachers, *Every Step of the Way: The Story of South Africa's Freedom* (Morris and Linnegar 2004).

- A set of six short books called *Turning Points in South African History* that cover crucial issues in South African history, from colonialism through apartheid (Nasson and Siebörger 2004). These books are also for high school students and teachers.
- The UNESCO *General History of Africa*, comprising eight volumes, with an updated volume and educator's guide, *Africa Since 1990*, by South African scholars (UNESCO, no date).
- A collection of essays, *Toward New Histories in South Africa*, a significant volume for reflecting on new opportunities for historical research and education (Jeppie 2004).
- An engaging and vividly illustrated book for children, *From Darkness to Light: Before and after Freedom*, which tells the story of life before and after democracy (cited in Asmal 2004).
- Maps, calendars, posters, and other learning materials.

From the abovementioned titles, it is clear that a new perspective is visible in these new publications. Although it took 10 years, South Africa's history textbooks have begun to reflect the democratic realities of the country.

Afrikaans Textbooks

The myth of Afrikaans as a unique, white creation with an independent branch of nonwhite speakers was propagated for an extended period, contributing to the distortion of Afrikaner values and attitudes. Exclusivity, color, and history were elevated by the myth, while universal values, merit, and individuality were downplayed. In fact, according to Statistics South Africa (2001), Afrikaans is the home language of 217,606 blacks, 2,931,489 "coloureds," 15,135 Indians, and 2,558,956 whites.

The caricature created by the myth led to difference becoming the norm. In a strongly worded comparison of the two most used first-language Afrikaans textbooks—*Afrikaans My Taal* and *Taalstudie vir die Middelbare Skool*—Esterhuyse (1986) demonstrated how apartheid Afrikaans language textbooks reflected a white, Afrikaner-centered approach in which Afrikaans was evidenced as the sole possession of a single group—the only group recognized in the choice of reading passages, naming, and examples. Speakers who deviated from the white Afrikaans standard were labeled "inferior" and "uncivilized." Esterhuyse (1986) and Webb (1992) also refer to the attempt in textbooks to portray the language of the "coloured Afrikaners" as only coarse and humorous, thereby reinforcing the clown or "jolly Hottentot" stereotype, as well as the race-related master symbol that explicates white supremacy.

The textbooks' silence concerning religious variety and the religious customs of other population groups was based on the Christian National Education system of the apartheid era. That system linked race and religion and was the mainspring of the privileged school system for whites in South Africa. In Du Preez's (1983) research, religious themes were found to emphasize God's prominence at all levels of Afrikaner life—individual, family, and government. Calvinism, the religious doctrine of the Afrikaner, barely accommodated other doctrines. Other doctrines are referred to incidentally in the textbooks examined by Du Preez, but those textbooks contain no evidence that God acknowledges such doctrines. God, therefore, is portrayed only in relation to the "white Afrikaner," reinforcing the notion of the exclusiveness of that relationship.

The publication of *Ruimland* (Botha and others 1989) helped pave the way for a new hidden curriculum in a democratic and multiracial South Africa.[4] Racial representation in the *Ruimland* textbook series was regarded as a major event for at least two reasons. First, Tony Links, then head of the Afrikaans Department of the University of the Western Cape, was the first ever co-author of color of an Afrikaans textbook. Second, it was possible to link the title of the series to a citation in the conclusion of Esterhuyse's 1986 work. The citation was derived from a poem by Hein Willemse, a poet and academic:

> Ons moet hierdie ruimland
>
> Waar mensheid verwar word
>
> Opbreek
>
> En van nuuts af oopbou.[5]

Complaints about the book were lodged in the press by the Conservative Party, a right-wing political party known to rely heavily on white Afrikaner support and whose policy defended apartheid principles and values. A Conservative Party member even called for the withdrawal of the *Ruimland* series after quoting from it during a government assembly:

> Today I urgently appeal to the honorable Minister of Education and Culture. . . . If this is not enough, I wish to call on the honorable State President to immediately withdraw this book from the eyes, thoughts and ears of our children (Jacobs 1991).

Why all this fuss? The traditional white Afrikaner felt threatened by the series at a time of great political uncertainty. First, *Ruimland* represented a major ideological shift from the apartheid perspective of previous textbooks, offering a socio-linguistically accurate picture of Afrikaans. As a first-language textbook, *Ruimland* was written for first-language speakers, of whom approximately 50 percent are "coloured Afrikaners." Second, the publication of *Ruimland* was the product of a battle against the master symbols of the past. Only rectifying racial representation to the core would bring about real change that would penetrate the circle of isolation and exclusivity brought about by those symbols. Third, *Ruimland* was an "awareness" series in the highly politicized era just before the dismantling of apartheid. Ideological patterns regarding change emerged to break the stereotypical perceptions that for so had long been at the core of enforced racial segregation in South Africa. According to one of the authors of the *Ruimland* series,

> It changed the whole perspective on the teaching of Afrikaans and even the perspective on Afrikaans as a language. What now goes without saying, was at that stage the starting point of it all (Pienaar 2003).

---

[4]Ruimland can be loosely translated as "spacious, expansive country/landscape."
[5]"This spacious country must be broken down and built anew (and open)."

The series operated as a sociocultural agent that provided a new formal, hidden, and null curriculum that led to the counter-creation of stereotypes. It could be regarded as an official curriculum that selected formal and explicit knowledge. Since the old curriculum, which preceded the current institutionalized South African curriculum, was based on the apartheid principle of exclusivity, it no longer was in touch with the demands of the "new South Africa." *Ruimland* overtly opposed exclusivity in textbooks and, as a hidden curriculum, taught society new behavior, values, and expectations. Furthermore, as a null curriculum, it intentionally moved away from Afrikaner master symbols to imbue students with democratic values.

> We thought children and teachers don't even know that they don't know; that's why we will develop a textbook to curb ignorance—it was almost a type of affirmative action (Pienaar 2000).

The fact that the series was a bestseller for years after the polemic that followed its publication could indicate a shift in the ideological world of the Afrikaner away from the apartheid master symbols.

Lessons Learned

What are the lessons learned in South Africa regarding textbooks? As far as Afrikaans language textbooks are concerned, it seems that the battle against racial stereotyping has been won. Assuming that traces of sociopolitical developments could be found in recent textbooks, Kusendila (2003) set out to compare the most recent Flemish and Afrikaans textbooks in terms of national identity. Her study suggests that in contexts of great national change, such as the abolition of apartheid in South Africa, the textbook can offer a platform for different, even contradictory, values to help create a new cultural and social reality. The new Afrikaner looks to the future for unity while also remembering the divisive past; the old apartheid Afrikaner now becomes the "other" (Kusendila 2003: 14, 92). Kusendila finds that *Raamwerk* (Traut and others 2001) promotes a new Afrikaner, a reinvented "self" among "others," respectful and aware of diversity and valuing that awareness. Furthermore, *Raamwerk* reveals a highly inclusive South African nationality and inclusive multiculturalism based on "unity through diversity." If this is true, the Afrikaans language textbook landscape in the first post-apartheid decade has changed rapidly in negotiating and constructing ways to deal with the new democracy.

However, history textbooks have not shown the same immediate transformation as Afrikaans textbooks. In the first years after apartheid was dismantled, the sentiment was that "it is better not to have history at all than to have that kind of history." We now know that history can be (mis)used for exclusive identity, but we also know that that approach makes negative history. Everything from the past that contradicts the required self-esteem of the white in-group is ignored; identity then becomes unchanging, oblivious of the effect of time and experience. We are more than aware now that simplistic, self-absorbed, and unified narratives cannot be socially relevant—even if they are told this time from the other side's perspective. Historical difference lies at the heart of historical relevance; otherwise, history can never become a memory bank of cultural resources (Tosh 2002, cited in Polakow-Suransky 2002).

Kader Asmal concluded his March 2004 address by emphasizing the need for historical difference or, as he called it, *inclusive memory*:

Forging our future required remembering our past. "One who wants to create the future," Anton Lembede said, "must not forget the past." Significantly, Anton Lembede was quoting from the "Political Testament" of the Boer leader, Paul Kruger, who had said that whoever "dares to create a future must not forget the past." In our inclusive memory of the South African past, the legac[ies] of leaders such as Paul Kruger or Anton Lembede belong to all of us. They cannot be owned by any exclusive or sectional interests in our society. They cannot be used to divide us. So, we need an inclusive memory of the past for a unified South Africa.

We also have learned that history is vital in the rebuilding of formerly authoritarian societies. There are stories to be told to ensure "the widest possible definition of memory and to make the process of recall as accurate as possible so that our knowledge of the past is not confined to what is immediately relevant" (Tosh 2000 in Polakow-Suransky 2002). Again, to quote Asmal:

In Africa, in the struggle between the hunter and the lion, the hunter has written the history. The lion, we have always hoped, will one day have its day. The lion will one day have its say. The lion will one day rise up and write the history of Africa. We know, very well, the kinds of histories that have been written by the hunter. Those books only serve the hunter's interests. But those books are so often also boring and stultifying. We now want to hear the lion's story. We now want to hear the lion's roar.

References

Apple, M. W. 1990. *Ideology and Curriculum*. New York: Routledge.

Apple, M. W., and L. K. Christian-Smith, eds. 1991. *The Politics of the Textbook*. New York: Routledge Roland.

Asmal, K. 2004. "Keeping Memory Alive, Shaping our Future: The Ten-Year Celebration of Freedom. Address by the minister of education, Centre for the Book, Cape Town. March 31. Available at http://www.info.gov.za/speeches/2004/04040109461001.htm.

Auerbach, F. E. 1965. *The Power of Prejudice in South African Education*. Cape Town: Gothic Printing.

Bam, J. 2000. "Negotiating History, Truth, Reconciliation, and Globalization: An Analysis of the Suppression of Historical Consciousness in South African Schools as Case Study. *Mots pluriels* (April 13): 1–13.

Botha, K., J. Esterhuyse, R. Gouws, T. Links, and J. Pienaar. 1989. *Ruimland 8*. Cape Town: Maskew Miller Longman.

———. 1990. *Ruimland 9 and 10*. Cape Town: Maskew Miller Longman.

Bundy, T. 1993. "What Makes a Nation Happy? Historiographical Changes and the Implication for Textbooks." Paper delivered at the Sparkling Waters seminar on school history textbooks for a democratic South Africa. Rustenburg, South Africa.

Chernis, R. E. 1990. "The Past in the Service of the Present: A Study of South African History Syllabuses and Textbooks 1839–1990." Unpublished Ph.D. diss. University of Pretoria.

Department of Systematic Theology and Theological Ethics. 2000. "Tutorial Letter 2001: Human Rights, Values, and Social Transformation." Part 2. Faculty of Theology and Religious Studies, University of South Africa, Pretoria.

Du Plessis, H., and T. Du Plessis, eds. 1987. *Afrikaans en taalpolitiek, 15 opstelle.* Pretoria: HAUM.

Du Preez, J. M. 1983. *Africana Afrikaner: meestersimbole in Suid-Afrikaanse skoolhandboeke.* Alberton: Librarius Felicitas.

Esterhuyse, J. 1986. *Taalapartheid en skoolafrikaans.* Emmarentia: Taurus.

Higgs, P., ed. 1995 *Metatheories in Educational Theory and Practice.* Sandton: Heinemann.

History Education Group. 1993. *History Matters.* Houghton: Heinemann-Centaur.

Jacobs, F. 1991. Republic of South Africa National Assembly debate. June 3. Cape Town.

Jansen, J. D. 1997. "Critical Theory and the School Curriculum." In *Metatheories in Educational Theory and Practice,* ed. P. Higgs (129–39). Sandton: Heinemann.

Jeppie, S., ed. 2004. *Toward New Histories for South Africa: On the Place of the Past in Our Present.* Landsdowne: Juta Gariep.

Joubert, C. J., and J. J. Britz. 1975. *History for Standard 10.* Johannesburg: Perskor.

Kusendila, B. 2003. "Language Education and National Identity: A Comparative Study of Flemish and Afrikaans L1 Instruction Materials since 2000." Unpublished M.Ed. diss. University of Cape Town.

Marsden, W. E. 2001. *The School Textbook: Geography, History, and Social Studies.* London: Woburn Press.

Morris, M., and M. Linnegar, ed. 2004. *Every Step of the Way: The Journey of Freedom in South Africa.* Cape Town: HSRC Press.

Nasson, B., and R. Siebörger. 2004. *Turning Points in History.* Johannesburg: STE Publishers.

Pape, J., Johanneson, Mashini, and Friedman. 1998. *Making History, Grade* 12. Sandton: Heinemann.

Pienaar, J. 2000. Interview with the author. June 25.

———. 2003. E-mail correspondence with the author. September 3.

Polakow-Suransky, S. S. 2002. "Historical Amnesia? The Politics of Textbooks in Post-Apartheid South Africa." Paper presented at the annual meeting of the American Educational Research Association, New Orleans, LA.

Seleti, Y., P. Delius, and G. Clacherty. 1999. *Looking into the Past, Grade 10.* Cape Town: Maskew Miller Longman.

Siebörger, R. 1992. "The Future of History Textbooks." Paper presented at the conference of the South African Society for History Teaching, Vista University, Pretoria, September 28–29.

Statistics South Africa 2000. "Stats in Brief 2000." Pretoria.

Strydom, F. 1997. "Die onderrig van Afrikaans in 'n geïdeologiseerde situasie." In *Taalkonteks*, ed. L. Combrink, N. Faasen, N. Geyser, and A. Kloppers (141–151). Pretoria: Juta.

Spencer, B. 1997. "Stereotypes and Language Proficiency: An Empirical Study." *Journal for Language Teaching*, 31(1): 51–67.

Tosh, J. 1991. *The Pursuit of History: Aims, Methods, and New directions in the Study of Modern History*. Essex: London.

Traut, J., R. Gouws, S. Peacock, and H. Snyman. 2001. *Raamwerk 10*. Cape Town: Maskew Miller Longman.

UNESCO. No date. "General History of Africa." 8 volumes. http://www.unesco .org/culture/africa/html_eng/index_en.htm. Accessed June 2005.

Van de Rheede, I. 1992. Die skool, Afrikaans en die kurrikulum. In *Afrikaans na apartheid*, ed. V.N. Webb (275–83). Van Schaik: Pretoria.

Van der Merwe, C. D. 2000. "Multi-Cultural Education: Panacea to Racism in the 21st Century." *Education Practice* 4: 28–34.

Webb, V. N. 1992. *Afrikaans na apartheid*. Pretoria: Van Schaik.

Willemse, Hein. 1986. Poem reproduced in *Taalapartheid en skoolafrikaans*, ed. J. Esterhuyse. Emmarentia: Taurus.

5

Romani Children in European Schools: Recent Experience

Maria Andruszkiewicz

Europe has long had a sizable Romani minority population, yet its students would be hard pressed, in school, to learn about the history, language, and culture of the Romani people. Despite a presence in Europe dating back 600 years, and a population numbering some 12 million worldwide, Romani history, languages and culture remain largely misunderstood.[1]

Majority School Curricula: The Invisible Roma

European schoolchildren manage to absorb information, much of it inaccurate, about a people still commonly called "gypsies." In fact, the Romanis' diverse and resilient culture is often warped into a body of folklore that would be dismissed as the worst kind of racism if applied to any other minority population. The canon of European folk and fairy tales (and in contemporary urban legend) depicts the Romani people as unreliable and often criminal nomads who, in the seventeenth century, stole chickens and kidnapped children and today filch wallets and mobile telephones.

Few school systems have introduced Romani folk tales, part of a rich oral tradition, into the curricula. Over the past decade, only a handful of accessible and informative texts have been developed on Romani culture, history, and language, and even these few resources are generally unavailable in schools.[2] It remains the case that educators working today, and most parents, have grown up with negative views about the Roma.

In most countries, less than 1 percent of Romani children complete higher education. Those who do complete university and go on to become credentialed teachers are typically assigned to schools with large Roma student populations. Although it is helpful for Romani schoolchildren to see adult Romani role models and teachers, the paucity of Romani educators means that majority schoolchildren continue to learn little about a sizable minority population. The few Romani teachers in the system are

---

[1]It is difficult to obtain accurate figures, as many Romani people do not declare themselves as such on census forms and in surveys. This report explains some of the reasons why they might not want to do so. The broad consensus is that Europe's Romani population is now approximately 8 million. There also are an estimated 1 million Roma living in the United States, and approximately 1.5 million Roma living in South America. Australia and Canada also have sizable Romani populations.

[2]Hancock (2002) includes suggestions for discussions and student projects that teachers can use.

rarely assigned to majority schools, so majority children rarely have their prejudices challenged by being taught by a teacher of Romani origin.

Consider this example from the Czech Republic. Although, according to estimates, there are between 250,000 and 300,000 Roma living in the Czech Republic (Lavicka 1998), the rest of society knows next to nothing about them—neither non-Roma nor Roma students learn about the minority in school.

Teachers of Romani origin who seek to address this ignorance can encounter obstacles of their own. A Bulgarian Romani said she imagined, as a teacher, she would be able "to combat this basic injustice" (Vassileva 1998). After graduating from university with distinction, she had the right, as she explains, "to opt for three schools of my choosing. Yet the municipal authorities pretended to have lost my application documents," she says, and then insisted she "teach in a 'gypsy school,' where, apparently, I belonged."

But she persisted and finally was assigned in a school with a majority Bulgarian population. She recalls the resistance she encountered there: "At every staff meeting I was made to feel guilty for being Roma. The school authorities even made it understood that I was the one to blame for the increase of Romani kids in the school." With her dream of an inclusive teaching environment dashed, the young teacher wondered if she had been wrong in not going to what others saw as her "'natural' school"—one with an enrollment of 90 percent Roma students (Vassileva 1998).

Although intercultural education is increasingly popular in Europe, Romani children still confront persistent ignorance from school administrators and teachers about their families, the communities, and their culture. There are strong arguments for adapting and enhancing curricula to build strong self-esteem and self-identity in Romani children. But without a retooled curricula—that challenge the hurtful stereotypes about the Roma and other minority populations—such initiatives will be wasted.

How "Special Educational Needs" Became "Reduced Curricula": A Brief History

Under communist regimes in central and eastern Europe, where most of the continent's Romani communities were concentrated in the twentieth century, efforts to improve access to education in general meant that educational opportunities for Romani children also improved. For example, in Bulgaria in the 1950s and 1960s, new schools were built in the countryside and in poorer neighborhoods and those with large Romani populations. Full-employment policies and free preschool meant that more Romani children attended kindergarten and school. Before 1990 and the fall of communism, central and eastern Europe could boast of a higher proportion of Romani children in their schools than western Europe.

Before 1989, for example, an estimated 120,000 Romani children were attending school every year in Bulgaria. But by 1998, that number had dropped to approximately 50,000, although the school-age Romani population had increased (Kyuchukov 1998). The number of illiterate Roma in Bulgaria increased from 28,897 in 1992 to 46,406 in 2001 (Panayatova 2002). Whatever the failings of an education system that was geared, first and foremost, toward creating "good Communists," most of the Romani academicians, writers, politicians, and activists who advocate for Romani rights today are beneficiaries of communist education policies.

Yet during this period Romani children, along with children of other minorities, were being educated under a strongly assimilationist education policy. Behaviors rooted in different cultural assumptions, and unfamiliarity with the language of instruction and with books and other teaching tools were identified ultimately, as deficiencies for which they had no pedagogical solutions.

In several countries, Roma children were eventually driven out of majority and mainstream schools or resorted to concealing their Roma identity. Svetlana Vassileva (1998), the Bulgarian teacher quoted above, describes how Romani children were automatically characterized as difficult and how the principal of her school sought to depress the enrollment of Roma children:

> Gradually more Roma families from the neighborhood decided they wanted to give their children a better education. The school authorities tried hard indeed to prevent the increase of Roma pupils. . . . One could hear, "I have enough Gypsies in my class," and "My class is too big as it is."

Vassileva concedes she became accustomed to routine Bulgarian bias against the Roma. "What was particularly painful to me," she adds, "was that the same banal prejudice was shared by my fellow teachers."

During the post–World War II period in central and eastern Europe, an increasing number of Romani children were educated in so-called gypsy schools. Although central and eastern Europe did not officially espouse segregated schools, certain schools (often in neighborhoods with significant Romani populations) were unofficially designated as gypsy schools, with poorer facilities, fewer resources, and lower-quality teaching than that found in majority schools. Recent research in rural schools in Romania found that in those schools with student enrollments of 50 percent or more Romani, more than half were less than three kilometers from schools with better facilities; such schools had a predominantly majority enrollment (Surdu 2002).

Research in Bulgaria also demonstrates that children themselves are aware of a deliberate, albeit unofficial, segregation. "They won't tell you," explains one Romani student in a Roma school, "that they don't want the child because you are a Gypsy. They will tell you that there are no vacancies. How can you check if this is true or not? Who can you complain to?" (Save the Children 2001).

The Romanian report cited above also found that overcrowded classrooms were three times more likely in primary schools with high Romani enrollments; this figure soars to nine times more likely in secondary schools with similar Romani enrollment. Two-thirds of schools with a preponderance of Romani pupils had no library or resource center. Given the high incidence of poverty and unemployment in Romani communities, parents and students cannot afford to buy books and other educational resources. School libraries are therefore vital for disadvantaged students if they are to keep up with their reading and study for examinations. As one Romani parent explains in Bosnia Herzegovina: "I cannot provide the school books. . . . Also, you see [gesturing inside the house] that there is no space for them to study" (Save the Children 2001).

Many Romani communities, particularly in Europe, are struggling with extremely high levels of poverty and unemployment in addition to crowded homes with inadequate (and sometimes nonexistent) heat, electricity, and plumbing. Libraries and after-school programs or homework clubs—any place that provides a secure, quiet after-school place to study—are vital for disadvantaged children. At present, out-of-school support of this kind is provided to only a few thousand children, usually by nongovernmental organizations (NGOs) that rely on grants from external donor agencies to cover their running costs. This reliance on nonstate finance and external aid leaves many such schemes in a precarious financial situation. They are time-bound "aid" projects, rather than a component of education provision that is available to all children who need such support. Schools in which the majority of pupils are Romani also are much more likely to have unqualified teachers. Surdu's report on conditions in Romanian schools asserts that in 1998, unqualified teachers were present "in every rural school" that had Romani enrollments of more than 50 percent. The director of a primary school in Macedonia described the conditions he found on taking up his post. The school was built to accommodate 800 pupils but had 2,000 instead—only 2 of whom are non-Romani. "I was shocked," he said, adding that the school had no windows, "the classroom doors were broken and so were most of the desks and chairs. There was not enough school equipment and the sanitary conditions were very alarming. I didn't know where to start" (Save the Children 2001).

Given the resources kept from Romani children in "gypsy schools," it is reasonable to assume that Romani children will have little access either to materials or to teaching methodologies that will build either self-esteem or pride in their ethnic identity. Poor facilities and unqualified teachers cannot combat social and economic disadvantage or accommodate non-native speakers of the language of instruction.

One Bulgarian student enrolled in a so-called Roma school said, when interviewed, "You can't learn anything in this school. There aren't enough rooms and we study in three shifts. The teachers don't care. Anyone who manages to get into a 'Bulgarian school' almost always graduates, while here only a few students finish 8th grade every year."

Another remarked: "They give you a C grade whether you know the subject or not, just to get rid of you. There are some students here in the fifth grade [who] can't even read. The teachers send you to do their shopping for them and you don't have to come back to class afterwards" (Save the Children 2001).

Non-native speakers lose their incentive to learn when the curriculum does not accommodate their language differences, and when teachers are not trained to work with them. A Croatian Romani girl observed:

> I can understand Croatian well and I understand what they are saying to me, but I can't answer them so that they understand me; I don't speak clearly enough. This is very difficult for me, because they think I don't know anything although that isn't true. It's easier for me to do drawing instead. But I want to be a policewoman when I grow up.[3]

In majority schools staffed by non-Roma teachers, the most disturbing response to Romani children's perceived "deficiencies" has been the policy of removing these to so-called special schools for the mentally disabled. Throughout central and eastern Europe, a medical rather than social model of disability has prevailed for decades. This model has led to institutions and special schools being established for children with a range of real or perceived disabilities.[4] For example, a 1998 report

---

[3]Croatian child, quoted in Save the Children (2001).
[4]Save the Children (2001) documents high numbers of Romani children in special schools in Bulgaria, Czech Republic, Hungary, Serbia, and Slovakia.

on the Czech Republic stated that "up to 80 percent of all Romani children go to Special Schools" (Czech Helsinki Committee 1997). In some Hungarian special schools, 90 percent of the students are Roma.

Special schools offer what is called a "reduced" curriculum to students who are perceived to have learning difficulties or mild mental disabilities. Students at these schools receive no educational credentials and are consequently barred from advancing to higher education and training in some professions and from applying for senior management positions.

In addition, special school graduates may progress only to certain kinds of vocational training.[5] A 20-year-old Romani woman recently returned to Basic School II in the Slovakian town of K, only with a happenstance intervention. As a girl, she had been transferred from Basic School II to a special school. From there she had progressed to a Secondary Training School for waitresses and cooks, an institution that offered no opportunity to sit for the final exam, which if she passed it, would have allowed her to go to university and gain a valuable educational credential. This in turn would help her develop her career toward a management position with a good salary.

The happenstance intervention? Her request was approved because the school's vice-director was married to an employee of the Special Remedial School and had been persuaded of the young woman's abilities.

> My husband taught her at the Special Remedial School for the Mentally Handicapped. He told me that this girl is very talented and has above-average IQ. Her only problem was that her parents were completely uneducated people and could not support her and help her in preparation for school. . . . Her mother had six children, and upon the recommendation of the school and the Director, she agreed to be sterilized. However, the mother could not help her children with their education. She could not tell the time, for example.[6]

Children's removal from mainstream education and into special schools with reduced curricula and prospects often occurs after the child has been subjected to a culturally and linguistically biased IQ test. Children who are not proficient in the language used for the test are categorized as intellectually deficient, as are those who give what test-givers consider the wrong answer. A Serbian school psychologist reveals the cultural bias at the heart of one test question:

> [Romani students] don't understand the test questions and have no work ethic. . . . For example, I ask a child what he should do if he sees smoke coming out of a house. The right answer is that he would call the fire brigade or tell an adult. . . . Roma children as a rule reply that the stove should be cleaned or the stovepipe fixed to stop it smoking. Then I have to fail the child.[7]

IQ testing is sometimes dispensed with altogether. In most countries with a special school system, Romani parents who complain about racial slurs and bullying

---

[5] Taken from interviews conducted for Save the Children (2001).

[6] The researcher did not ask how this sterilization would have supported her children's study efforts. Many of the interviews conducted by Save the Children suggested contempt on the part of school staff for Romani children's parents and families ("uneducated" and "oversized" were commonly used terms). Also note that the vice-director absolves the school of any responsibility for nearly destroying the life-chances of an evidently intelligent and determined young woman.

[7] Interview conducted for Save the Children (2001).

are told to send their children to a special school. Why? Their child would have an easier time at a special school because so many Romani children were enrolled there. Some children's experiences in mainstream schools were so bad that they even volunteered for special school, as in this case of a young Czech Romani man (Lavicka 1998), now in his twenties:

> Children at school called me a "stinking Gypsy" and plugged their noses when I was around. Nobody wanted to talk to me. During gym, nobody wanted to stand next to me. My first reaction was to deny my identity. Soon after, I began to assert that I wasn't a Gypsy but Hungarian. I always went home in tears, received poor marks, and I wanted to go to a Special School because I knew that Romani children were in the majority there. My parents wanted me to study, however, so they kept me in the normal elementary school.

Not all parents are so determined or well informed. Many parents do not understand the damage to their children's prospects caused by a special education and its reduced curriculum.

Another disturbing phenomenon is the widely reported practice of special school staff who recruit pupils in Romani neighborhoods, promoting their easy curriculum but neglecting to say that its graduates are barred from proceeding either to university or a management position. Special school recruiters also exploit the poverty of many Romani communities. One 14-year-old Bulgarian Romani student explains that special school teachers "come here every fall and go around the neighborhood telling people to send their children there because it is like a boarding school and they won't have to worry about clothing or feeding them. . . . And the poorer people agree. They can't help it."[8]

Some Romani parents also described the difficulty of reversing a special school placement decision and decried the way their children were pressured to lobby their parents about keeping them in special schools: "They are being educated according to the shortened program," one Croatian Romani mother said, "like the one for children with learning difficulties. And then, later on, they will have problems if they want to enroll in secondary school. Children are told that this is best for them. . . . We feel powerless."

The arguments advanced by the proponents of special schools are instructive. A Czech journalist (Sabotka and Uhlova 1998) noted that they were voiced by those who work in the schools: "Special Schools are sufficient for Romani pupils," they said, *"because afterwards there is a possibility of getting vocational training."*[9] School staff conceded, in addition, that Romani children in special schools would be "among children from their own culture and under the supervision of sympathetic and *unprejudiced*[10] pedagogues."[11]

---

[8] Elena Marushiakova and Vessilin Popov carried out this interview for Studii Romani, which published their findings in Save the Children (2001). Studii Romani produces publications on the history, culture, and languages of southeastern European Roma.

[9] Emphasis supplied. The use of "sufficient" here is interesting, as is the assumption that vocational training is the most that Romani young people can reasonably aspire to.

[10] Italics mine. This is an interesting early admission that school staff and school authorities were aware that Romani children were being driven out of mainstream schools because of teachers' racist views and behaviors.

[11] Sobotka went on to become a committed advocate and activist for Romani children's rights.

Data collected in recent United Nations Development Programme (UNDP) household surveys show the ease with which Roma parents are persuaded to place their children in special schools (UNDP 2003). Of Romani parents interviewed whose children attend a special school, 76 percent of Czech parents, 49 percent of Hungarian parents, and 41 percent of Bulgarian parents said that the easier program was an incentive for them. The percentages of these parents whose children had actually been diagnosed as disabled were somewhat different: 54 percent in Bulgaria, 31 percent in Czech Republic and Slovakia, 58 percent in Romania, and 49 percent in Hungary.

Efforts to desegregate the Bulgarian Gypsy school system have met with opposition from all-Romani schools. An activist at the forefront of the desegregation movement in Bulgaria, Donka Panayotova recounts that the director of an all-Romani school, backed by municipal authorities: "attempted to obstruct the desegregation process by refusing to give Romani children certificates to leave the school. Without these certificates, children cannot attend another school." She also reports that school staff feared the loss job security that would come with the loss of Romani students, observing that "some teachers at the school, because of their poor qualifications, were unlikely to find jobs in any other school in town."

The formal response to the desegregation project? A decision that banned departing Romani children from ever returning to the Gypsy schools (Panayotova 2002).

As it happens, Romani children involved in the desegregation project did initially encounter academic and other difficulties when they entered majority schools. These difficulties suggest that the all-Roma schools, like the special schools, offered a reduced curriculum to their disadvantaged Romani pupils.

During their first year in majority schools, Romani children needed intensive support, extra lessons, and summer and winter study camps to reach the level of their non-Romani peers. But they rose to the challenge. Students who had frequently missed school in the past amassed excellent attendance records in their new schools, and none of the newly integrated Romani children had to repeat the school year due to poor grades.

Finally, in this brief overview of Roma school curricula we should note that, in some parts of central and eastern Europe, Romani children constituted a very high proportion of children in residential care institutions. Under communism and well into the 1990s, child protection authorities favored a "rescue and remove" policy toward children living in poverty, born out of wedlock, or in "disorganized" families (those, for example, with a parent in jail or with drug or alcohol problems). Anecdotal evidence suggests that Roma children were actively recruited by institutional staff, in reference to the rescue and remove policy. They stressed the economic benefits institutionalized children would receive in the form of free food, clothing, and school materials. Some institutions, especially those for disabled children, also educated children in-house.

In the mid-1990s Save the Children worked with young people who had been institutionalized in Bulgaria. It found the children were poorly equipped for life outside an institution. They had few qualifications and lacked necessary life skills, for example, to shop for groceries, cook, manage a household budget, and look for a job. They are overrepresented in correctional institutions and are also vulnerable to exploitation, including trafficking.

Given the many Romani children institutionalized in Bulgaria, Hungary, Romania, and elsewhere, more research needs to be done on educations offered there.[12] The particular disadvantages of growing up apart from their families require more than rehabilitation. They require education in critical thinking and life skills that will help to protect them from harm and exploitation.[13]

The "Reduced" Curriculum and Its Consequences for Romani Students: Vocational Training

"I would like to be a teacher. My mum wants me to change schools, because she says that is the only way for me to become a teacher."

—*Romani girl, 11 years, attending a special school for mentally handicapped*[14]

"I would never, ever, return to that [Romani-only] school. I have a dream to become a lawyer and I think that my new school will help me to achieve that."

—*Romani boy who benefited from Vidin desegregation project, now in fifth* grade[15]

Educational provision for Romani children *and* perceptions of the Roma among majority and other minority groups would certainly improve if there were more Romani teachers, school directors, writers of educational materials, civil servants, and policymakers.

The legacy of low expectations, however, has channeled Romani children into special schools and "Gypsy schools"—both burdened with poor facilities and reduced curricula. These inherent disadvantages, together with the cost of higher education and professional training, make Romani parents reluctant to spend time and resources, especially given labor market discrimination. So, regardless of their interests or abilities, Romani children are directed toward vocational education. For example, in Hungary, upon completing basic school, students can progress either to an academic grammar school or to a vocational school to learn a trade. Fewer than 3 percent of Romani young people opted for grammar school. In addition, Romani participation in tertiary education is practically nil, estimated at less than 0.1 percent.[16]

---

[12]Although, because the recording of ethnic origin is officially forbidden in many of these countries, we still must rely on anecdotal reports from organizations and people who have worked in such institutions, including NGOs and agencies like UNICEF.

[13]Most central and eastern European countries that have overrelied on institutional care now acknowledge this practice often severely impedes the physical and emotional development of children. As a consequence, substantial efforts have been made to replace institutional models with foster care, adoption, and family support programs to prevent children from being taken into the care of the state. In the case of adoption, domestic antipathy toward Roma makes foreign adoption the best option for Romani children. Most Romani families are too poor to foster or adopt an orphaned or abandoned Romani child. Only a few non-Romani parents foster Romani children in their native countries, and most adoptive and foster parents prefer infants and toddlers. Romani children abandoned by desperately poor parents in the late 1980s and early 1990s are now too old to be chosen for adoption or foster care.

[14]Interviewed in 2000 for Save the Children (2001).

[15]Quoted in Panayotova (2002).

[16]Save the Children 2001. In Montenegro in 2001, only three Romani students went on to high school out of an estimated Romani population of 20,000.

Vocational training for young Roma generally equips them for low-status jobs (for example, car mechanics, hairdressers, and machine operators). They are also educated as para-professionals (classroom assistants, healthcare workers). It would seem a simple matter for a classroom assistant to apply her work experience toward credits for a teaching credential, or for health visitors to receive additional training that would qualify them as nurses. Professional status is jealously guarded, however, particularly in postcommunist states. Awarding professional credentials based on demonstrated competence is a relatively new idea there, though it is gaining ground. In the meantime, emphasis continues on the years of completed formal education. "Access courses" are almost unheard of.[17]

Similarly, "modular" and "open" learning courses, which enable students to vary the pace of their studies and allow them to work and study, are also rare. In general, higher education courses start and finish on fixed dates. For students, or would-be students, on small budgets, requirements that dictate when and how they should study can be too onerous to bear. For example, would-be students working in the agricultural sector or in low-paying jobs (who must work overtime or take a second job in the event of a family illness) require flexible academic schedules if they are to get any additional schooling.

Affirmative action programs in high schools and universities have achieved good results, especially when combined with scholarships and subsidized housing for economically disadvantaged students. But these programs are available to only a small number of determined and fortunate Romani young people who have managed to graduate from high school.

Signs of Hope: New Policy and Practice, NGO Innovation, and Government Reform

Since the mid-1990s and the post-transition period, the marginalization of central and eastern Europe's Romani communities has become more widely known. Institutions such as the European Union, Council of Europe, and the Organization for Security and Co-operation in Europe's Office for Democratic Institutions and Human Rights (ODIHR/OSCE) began to devote increasing attention to Roma. The agency has frequently named education as a priority if the region is to prevent the emergence of a permanently marginalized Roma underclass excluded from the benefits of post-transition economic growth.

The difficult economic conditions of the early postcommunist transition prompted international donors and aid and development agencies to respond to the needs of the poorest and most underserved. At the same time, efforts to promote civil society and build capacity of newly emerging NGOs gave human rights activists an opportunity to draw attention to the plight of the Roma. They publicized cases of institutionalized discrimination and abuse and argued that these were worsening the Roma's social and economic isolation in newly democratic states of Europe.

---

[17] In 2003 the Pedagogical High School in Cluj Napoca, Romania, established a training course for school mediators under the Access to Education for Disadvantaged Groups project. In the event some mediators wish to train as teachers, the school director is investigating ways for applicants to contribute credits toward a teaching qualification upon completion of mediator training.

As a consequence, international donors, governments, and NGOs began to fund a vast number of Roma-related initiatives. For example, in Hungary between 1990 and 1999, approximately 1,400 Roma projects were funded in the fields of health, education, housing, and employment. Initially, governments were reluctant to acknowledge that truancy and poor educational outcomes among Romani children were the result of anything other than poverty. So-called educational programs targeting Romani children tended to focus on alleviating some material disadvantages by providing free school meals. Because so many Romani children go to school hungry, these meal programs provide incentive for children from the poorest families to attend school on a regular basis.[18]

In some countries, economic barriers continue to prevent many Romani children from getting an education (UNDP 2003). In Romania half the Roma parents interviewed said their children had no presentable clothes for school; more than a quarter of Bulgarian Roma parents reported the same, like their Romanian counterparts citing this as a principal reasons for keeping their children from school. In Bulgaria 46 percent of Roma parents interviewed said that the provision of food, clothing, and shelter was the main reason they sent their children to a special school.

Before governments address important curriculum and pedagogical issues, and before Romani children even enter mainstream and integrated classrooms, the Roma must overcome a host of economic, environmental, and social obstacles. Roma settlements tend to be in isolated areas underserved by transport links; this also makes trips to and from school difficult, and dangerous, in bad weather.

Models of Good Practice

The introduction of new legislative frameworks and the efforts of international and domestic human rights activists produced broad government acknowledgment that Romani children have the right to be educated in mainstream, integrated schools.[19] This in turn has resulted in more attention to important curricular and pedagogical issues, including the sometimes subtle ways in which Romani children are excluded. There is, in short, growing awareness that barriers to education go beyond poverty; this awareness has resulted in new policies and practices being piloted in several European countries.

The first initiatives were small-scale projects run by NGOs and funded by outside donors rather being part of state education budgets. Because they operated parallel to the formal education system, they had a negligible impact on the system as a whole. Only in the past few years have state education systems started to draw on what has become a sizable laboratory of innovation to institute reforms. Most of these initiatives have been in place for only a few years, and so cannot be fully eval-

---

[18]In household surveys conducted by UNDP (2003), 37 percent of Roma families in Bulgaria and 33 percent in Romania consider themselves to be "constantly starving." The figures are much lower for the more developed economies of Czech Republic, Slovakia, and Hungary (4, 0.8, 1.7 percent respectively). When asked, however, if they were "never" in a situation where there was not enough to eat in the household, 68 percent of Czech respondents agreed; the figures for Roma in Slovakia and Romania were 65 and 62 percent, respectively.

[19]Both the Hungarian and Romanian governments are undertaking efforts to end school segregation of Romani children. For example, in 2004, the Romanian Ministry of Education issued a desegregation instruction to all school inspectorates with the aim of eliminating all forms of segregated schooling for Roma children within three years.

uated. But early indications are consistent about the kinds of change needed if schools are to be more welcoming and effective for Romani children and young people.

How to Begin? Literacy, Numeracy, and "School Survival Skills"

For many of the new educational initiatives, the first priority has been to persuade the youngest children not only to enroll in school but also to complete at least their primary education.

Efforts to increase school enrollment have included programs that aim to overcome material and economic barriers to school attendance: free school meals and writing materials, free transportation in bad weather, and clothing donations so that children are not shunned because of their appearance. Other schemes provide "citizens advice" services to overcome the bureaucratic barriers that some schools erect to limit the enrollment numbers of Romani children, such as complicated paperwork required to register a child in school (a powerful disincentive for parents with low levels of literacy). In one well-known case in Timisoara, Romania, these barriers were so unassailable that a Romani activist set up an unofficial school in her own apartment to teach children who were losing years of primary education while their parents struggled with increasingly senseless demands for documentation. At the beginning of the 1999 school year, she discovered that teachers at a nearby school were redirecting Romani children to enroll in her unofficial school, which she was still operating out of her home despite her many requests for use of classroom space.[20]

Programs that focused on dismantling material and bureaucratic obstacles succeeded, however, only in getting children onto school premises. Children's achievement continued to be low, and absenteeism was high. Schools in predominantly Roma neighborhoods showed particularly poor results. Children who had attended school for three or four years still could barely read or write.

On issues of curriculum and language, the picture is equally disheartening. With most of the poverty-related barriers dismantled, it was assumed that Romani students would function as majority schoolchildren. Why were they failing? An obvious difficulty was language skills: Romani schoolchildren were not proficient in the language of instruction when they entered primary school. At home they spoke another language or dialect. The assumption was that children would pick up the language of instruction in automatic fashion and catch up with their classmates. Yet the incomprehensibility of the entire school experience, in addition to the language barriers, was devastating the children's confidence and motivation.

Language programs were therefore developed to help Romani first-graders understand the language of instruction. Initially, for a range of reasons[21]—mainly having to do with resources—few schools were able or willing to offer instruction

---

[20]Additional details of this case are documented in OSCE (2000).

[21]Among these, the low numbers of qualified teachers, a lack of suitable texts, too few children to justify the cost of employing an extra teacher, not wishing to segregate Romani children, and the wide range of nonstandardized and noncodified dialects that children speak in some areas. Additionally, because children eventually would have to move to a majority language teaching environment, educators feared leaving them with a linguistic disadvantage at a later stage in their education.

in Romani even for younger children. In most countries with sizable Roma minorities, policymakers were gradually acknowledging that children acquire literacy more easily if these skills are introduced in the language they already speak. Because so few Roma were completing secondary school, few Romani-speaking teachers were available for such basic literacy classes. Meanwhile, majority teachers had no training, texts, or resources to support children to learn to read and write in their mother tongue first and then to transfer this knowledge to understanding a second language.

Policymakers were beginning to concede, in addition, that the school environment might not be familiar or even friendly to Romani children. With parents who had not attended school, or had left school after only a few years, Romani children could not be inculcated with traditional school culture (for example, being "seen and not heard"). Those who were as a consequence labeled as having "behavioral problems" merely were unaware of the rules governing "proper" behavior in a classroom setting. For example, some Romani children became distressed, and disruptive, when instructed to sit apart—in different rooms—from their brothers and sisters. Such Romani schoolchildren, with admirable ideals about family solidarity, were being punished because they had no notions about institutional behavior.

Ill-prepared and inflexible majority teachers continue to present a barrier to the full participation of Romani children in classroom activities. It was observed during a February 2003 field visit to a Bucharest school that children whose families were unable to supply drawing paper or crayons sat, ignored and unoccupied, while the teacher worked with the rest of the class.[22] Teachers were unable adapt certain aspects of the curriculum by, for example, changing an individual task into a group activity so that students with no paper and pencils could learn alongside their better-equipped peers. In the posttransition economies, in particular, teachers have been isolated from developments in teaching practice that have introduced child-focused and anti-bias approaches.

Teachers with no previous concept of an intercultural, anti-bias approach are gradually being exposed to new models. Schools are introducing new preservice and in-service teacher training programs that allow teachers to observe and adapt practice from successful models of multicultural classrooms. In most posttransition economies, however, intercultural, anti-bias approaches and methodologies are not yet part of preservice teacher training.[23]

In many countries, the deployment of Romani teaching assistants and mediators has helped to bridge the divide between both teachers and students and schools and communities. Mediators are outreach liaison workers for schools and Romani families. Their role combines traditional education advocacy with community development and social work. They are affiliated with the school but visible in the community, keeping abreast of problems that might prevent children from attend-

---

[22] Field visit, author's project team.

[23] In Romania, a new "Open Distance Learning" course commenced in October 2003. Designed to train teachers to work with Romani children in a more culturally sensitive and effective manner, the course contains modules on intercultural, anti-bias principles and practice; there's also a compulsory module for all trainees on Roma language, history, and culture. Under the "Access to Education for Disadvantaged Groups" project, all teachers in this school subsequently received training in inclusive education principles.

ing school or that affect their academic performance once they are enrolled. A Bulgarian school principal interviewed in 1999 for a report by the OSCE High Commissioner for National Minorities (OSCE 2000) explained that teachers are not trained in effective, sensitive ways to encourage Roma parents to support their children's education goals. He described their manner as "authoritarian" and recounted one teacher whose home visits, he said, were devoted to berating parents for having too many children.

A Spanish case of using Roma mediators gives an indication of how sensitive their role is and how easily they can lose a community's trust. Initially, the mediators were highly successful, reducing nonenrollment in primary education from 90 percent to 17 percent in one case. But when the regional authorities began to fine parents (by reducing welfare payments) for any truant children, the mediators were asked to explain the new program to the Roma community. Although the fines created an incentive for lower truancy rates among Romani schoolchildren, the program also transformed mediators—who had been grass-roots school advocates for Romani children—into truant officers.

Well-trained classroom assistants and school mediators are important, to be sure. But it is equally important that principals and teachers become equally well-trained in how to work with them. The Nova Skola Association in the Czech Republic was among the first NGO-led training initiatives, one that eventually gained government support. Its initial difficulties grew out of poorly trained teachers, not poorly trained assistants and mediators. For example, teachers expected assistants to carry out menial tasks and did not value the advice or opinions of mediators.[24] School mediators in Spain also became frustrated when their attempts to advise on curriculum content and teaching approaches were repeatedly disregarded. Informed by these experiences elsewhere in Europe, the current training course for school mediators in Romania includes a module on communication skills.

Renewed Focus on Preschool Schemes

The transition period in many countries in central and eastern Europe was characterized by cutbacks in public spending. Education spending fell, and investment in facilities was deferred. As buildings fell into disrepair, fuel subsidies were removed so the traditional large preschool institutions became too expensive to heat in the winter. Falling birth rates meant, in any case, that many of these buildings were too large for preschool populations.

In many countries, preschool provision was rationalized with the closure of preschools attended by only a few children. Charges were introduced for meals and other subsidies for disadvantaged preschoolers.

Preschool enrollment and attendance of Romani children have always tended to be lower than that of children from majority populations. Roma families are reluctant to hand over their four- and five-year-olds to majority-run institutions, preferring to care for them *en famille*—a cultural preference that also hikes dropout rates among the older girls, since they are needed at home to mind children. Roma attendance fell even more post-1990, and more Roma children began first grade with little exposure to majority languages or classroom rules.

---

[24]The Nova Skola case study appears in Save the Children (2001).

New initiatives were established, mainly in the nongovernmental sector, to build community confidence in preschool institutions, cover the costs of preschool attendance, and prepare children to enter school familiar with the language of instruction and school culture.

The Open Society Foundation's "Step by Step" programs were among the most successful and well-known of these initiatives. They offered high-quality child-centered programs that accommodated children at different developmental stages. A friendly preschool setting was used to develop parents as allies and resources in the education of their children. Parents were invited to contribute to the program by assisting teachers, supervising musical and other activities, and improving and maintaining the school premises.

In Slovakia a kindergarten established by Through the Children to the Families, a nongovernmental organization, was at first viewed as a gypsy kindergarten—a perception that made majority Slovak parents reluctant to enroll their children there. Within five years, however, the proportion of Roma/Slovak enrolled was 50:50 after the school garnered a reputation for excellence, with a committed and caring staff delivering high-quality programs.

It is now widely acknowledged that Romani children, in particular, need the opportunities offered in preschool to acquire the skills they will need if they are to succeed in primary school. Preschools also can offer a rewarding and enjoyable initial experience of structured learning and promote community involvement and trust in education. A preschool curriculum that welcomes Romani and other cultures in the form of music, paintings, and play materials is an early opportunity for parents, too, to see formal education in a positive light.

The Next Challenge: Keeping Children in School

Surveys on international good practice indicate that, even in traditional school settings with no intercultural instruction, children thrive when taught by committed, sensitive, and motivated teachers.

But Romani students and parents—and many school principals and teachers—emphasize the positive effects of incorporating Romani language, history, narratives, art, and music into curricula for *all* children. Romani schoolchildren certainly identify with the material but, perhaps more important, majority children have an opportunity to shed inaccurate preconceptions (which often so easily morph into racism) when minority cultures are addressed in the classroom. When Finland introduced Romani language and history in the curriculum, children who had previously appeared disaffected showed renewed interest in attending school (Advisory Board 1999). In Romania, in two of the pilot schools under the "Access to Education for Disadvantaged Groups" project, Romani language, literature, and culture classes have proved popular among majority Romanian children. In a number of the pilot schools, Romani parents, too, have asked to attend the classes.

All the examples of successful practice that have been documented have sought to make the school a visibly less alien environment for Romani children. For example, where few Roma have teaching credentials, schools can give Roma adults positions of authority by employing them as teaching assistants. Romani assistants are particularly important in the early grades of school to ensure that children who have yet to develop a strong command of the language of instruction can follow the curriculum.

At the Premysl Pitter Elementary School in Ostrava, Czech Republic—with a population that is 95 percent Roma—children who need extra language support also have access to a preprimary "grade zero" class where they can develop their language skills. Additional Czech-language instruction is available to all children for the first four grades.

Like those at preschool and secondary levels, all of the successful primary education initiatives make strenuous efforts to bring parents onto school premises and to foster a perception within the wider community that the school is a resource for adults as well as children. The Premysl Pitter School employs a social worker who helps families to deal with problems unrelated to education that might have a negative impact on children's school performance, for example, health and housing problems.

In many countries, an increase in the number of Roma children dropping out of school has been observed at "breaking points" in the school cycle, for example, when students transfer schools or move to a more demanding curriculum stage at age 11 or 12. For example, in Hungary in 1997, 62 percent of Hungarian students entered secondary school, while only 9 percent of Roma children did so.

More research is needed to understand the particular pressures exerted during these "breaking points." It has been suggested that the requirement for more homework and revision causes problems for children in overcrowded housing and that students who work after school find it hard to keep up, eventually losing heart and giving up on their educations. Furthermore, in countries in which innovations such as child-focused and anti-bias approaches were introduced in preschool and early grades first, children who progressed into "unreconstructed" grades of the school program rapidly lost their enthusiasm for school.

Need for More Books and Student Resources

Throughout Europe, a severe shortage of high-quality educational materials is hampering the effort to introduce the study of Roma language, history, narrative, and music into curricula. Good materials do exist, but their print-runs have been much too small to meet demand. In Greece, teachers who had used a language primer with success then ordered more copies from the Ministry of Education only to discover the book was out of print. In a survey of Romanian schools with high numbers of Romani students, researchers reported that, while some good materials had been produced, children almost never had access to them.[25] For example, teachers in Bacau had access to 60 copies of a Romani reading and writing manual, yet they needed more than 1,200 copies if students were to use it themselves. In surveyed schools in Mures County, three copies of a book of Romani songs were available, while teachers estimated they needed 2,500 if students were to benefit from learning (which is to say, reading) lyrics as an aid to literacy, rather than merely memorizing lyrics sung or spoken by teachers.

In most schools, the typical stock of student texts and teachers' materials reflects the invisibility most Romani children and young people experience in

---

[25] Ongoing work begun under the EU-funded project, Access to Education for Disadvantaged Groups with a Special Focus on Roma. Teachers, parents, and children also are involved in an EU-funded consultation to identify content for new educational materials.

majority settings. Romani schoolchildren are consigned to outsider status when their history, culture, and language are invisible in the classroom.

But new anti-bias texts and resources are being written and created, and this is a positive development. Nevertheless, more attention is needed to integrate Romani history and culture into texts and materials throughout the curriculum and for all children in countries with significant Roma populations.

Roma School Inspectors

One notable initiative may improve retention rates in Romanian schools. In 1999 the Ministry of Education appointed Roma school inspectors in every county (although, as yet, not all of these inspectors are Romani). Their role is to monitor enrollment and attendance, develop working relationships between schools and NGOs working on educational issues with Roma communities, guide schools on curricula and materials, and identify opportunities and assistance for Romani young people to advance to secondary schools. As with the first Romani classroom assistants and school mediators, there are concerns that the School Inspectorates may not adequately acknowledge the authority of Roma inspectors.

With support from the PHARE program, the European Union's financial and technical cooperation with the countries of central and eastern Europe, Roma inspectors will be trained in inclusive education principles and learn how to advise schools on antibias educational environments and curricular issues. These include the design of specific school-based curricula that reflect minority needs in particular schools. Under the same program, School Inspectorates participate in developing and piloting of a national school assessment tool. This evaluation instrument will assess inclusiveness, teaching practices, curriculum content, and the extent of community participation in school life.

Ending Segregation in Special Schools

The long-standing practice of segregating Romani children by enrolling them in schools for the disabled (so-called special schools) is one of the biggest reform challenges facing the Czech Republic, Hungary, and Slovakia; but the problem persists in Bulgaria and even Romania. Curriculum reform is essential because, as one former special education teacher, a Czech, explained, such a school, at best, prepares its students to be mere carpenter's assistants; they cannot even be professional carpenters (OSCE 2000).

In the Czech Republic, graduates of special schools were ineligible for mainstream secondary schools until late 1999, when the Chamber of Deputies amended the School Act to permit such enrollment if applicants pass the entrance examination. Hungary passed a similar law in 1992, but it made little practical difference. Allowing Roma children to take the secondary school entrance examination is one thing. It is another to ensure that they have the knowledge and skills to pass it. The reduced curriculum offered by special schools also reduces the likelihood that students so educated can master a mainstream curriculum.

An immense challenge awaits those countries that for decades relied on special schools to segregate a disadvantaged population, shirking responsibility for educating a sizable and underserved minority. The schools themselves, and the public's perception of them, must both be transformed.

A related challenge is to persuade Romani parents that their children can cope with and achieve in mainstream schools, studying a mainstream curriculum. One of the most pernicious legacies of the segregation of generations of Romani children is the resulting assumption that special schools provide the most appropriate educational environment for their children. An astonishing 76 percent of Czech Romani parents surveyed said they sent their children to a special school because "the programme is easier there and the child will cope with it."[26] Perceptions that teachers in special schools are thought to be more sensitive may also encourage Czech Roma parents. This admirable trait, sensitivity, could form a basis for the retraining of special school staff to teach a mainstream curriculum. Less optimistically, it indicates an immense task of teacher training and awareness raising in mainstream schools.

Of immediate concern in the transition/transformation of special schools is the amount of support children will need. It is hoped that children will respond positively to the new challenges. But, particularly with the older children, the fear is that some might find the gap is too great to bridge and that they will be overwhelmed by the ground they must recover, with the result that they will recoil from intellectual challenges in a new school setting.

The Step by Step Roma Special Schools Initiative, sponsored by the Open Society Institute (2004), is one of a handful of pilot projects addressing the transition. It evaluates the process and outcomes and documents the learning points. The project evaluation generated similar conclusions drawn by the Bulgarian desegregation project mentioned above—namely, that, given appropriate support and conditions, the majority of Roma children are capable of academic achievement in mainstream schools. After two years, 64 percent of children in the Step by Step pilot project were achieving at a level that permitted their integration into the mainstream system. It is interesting to note that children who entered grade 1 speaking only Romani were the most likely to achieve to this level, indicating that a strong background in home language can be an asset rather than a deficit if schools can develop strategies to build on children's existing language skills.

The Step by Step pilot makes clear recommendations that, if special schools are to make a successful transition to the mainstream, teachers, parents, and children require comprehensive support during the initial years. Staff and administrators involved in pilot expressed high expectations for Romani children after receiving the training and support that increased their confidence about delivering the mainstream curriculum. Not surprisingly, good teacher-student relationships were key in creating a positive attitude toward school; students with the most positive attitudes also reported that they liked their teachers and teaching assistants.

The project also employed Roma family coordinators, who acted as community-school mediators and advised on the incorporation of Roma language, culture, and history in the curriculum. The more parents were involved in the work of the school, the more they wanted their children to succeed in a mainstream setting. Ninety-eight percent of parents of grade 3 students, both in the pilot and at control sites, stated they believed that "school is important." Although only 14 percent of parents at project pilot sites hoped their children would move into a mainstream school, no parents in control sites had this expectation.

---

[26] Parent quoted in UNDP (2003).

Innovations in Secondary Schools

Given that so many Roma children do not complete primary school, primary education has been the focus of most recent initiatives. But recent innovations in secondary education should be noted. In 2000 the World Bank Regional Office in Hungary commissioned a review of alternative secondary-school models to document and evaluate some of these initiatives, which could serve as models for other countries (World Bank 2001). All of these initiatives were established in response to the perception that the state secondary education system was failing to meet the needs of minority Roma students and that Roma students were capable of achieving good educational results if a curriculum were adapted to meet their needs.

A particular problem at secondary school level has been the practice of educating Roma students mainly in vocational or technical schools rather than academic secondary schools (also called grammar schools or *gymnaziums* in some countries). In 1995 Hungary legislated a requirement that vocational students receive at least two years of mainstream (academic) education and have the option of taking the national examinations required for college or university entry. In addition, the type of vocational training offered was revised to make it more relevant to the changing job market. A similar revision of vocational training is underway in Romania.

Among the new models that have been developed in Hungary, the Collegium Martineum offers intensive academic and pastoral support and hostel facilities for 30 students aged 14–18. The Gandhi Public Foundation Secondary Grammar School and Students' Hostel is a secondary school offering a preparatory program for university entry. In 1999, 170 students aged 12–18 years followed the General Education curriculum along with Romani and Beash language instruction. (Beash is an archaic form of Romanian similar to the Székely dialect of Hungarian.) The school's mission is to create positive role models and eventually to contribute to the creation of a young Roma elite. The Kalyi Jag Roma Minority Professional School caters to secondary, vocational, and university students aged 14–25 and has a focus on more up-to-date vocational training such as information technology (IT) skills. In 1999 about 60 students who had completed primary school but not enrolled in secondary school—and now could not because of age restrictions—attended the school.

All of the new secondary-school models have a lower student-teacher ratio than mainstream secondary schools: 6:7 at Collegium Martineum, 5:6 at the Gandhi College, and 6:8 at Kalyi Jag, while the Hungarian national average for general secondary schools is 10:3.

In addition, teachers possess special qualifications or are getting additional training. When interviewed, most principals believed that basic teacher training did not provide a credential to teach, effectively, at Roma secondary schools. Familiarity with and knowledge of Roma culture were mentioned as additional requirements along with the ability to work in a student-centered and participatory manner; "emotional intelligence"—traits like sensitivity, creativity, open-mindedness—were also identified as important. Principals tended to prefer younger teachers who were willing to be flexible and creative over older, more experienced teachers who tended to be more rigid.

A "whole school approach" to creating an inclusive environment also was found to be important. At the Collegium Martineum, the housekeeper and kitchen supervisor, a Beash-speaking Roma, was an important resource as confidante and informal counselor to the students.

All of the schools surveyed had experienced steady enrollment hikes. Students reported that word of mouth from former teachers, friends, and relatives was important in encouraging them to enroll. Some of the students had never expected to return to school after leaving. Many cited racism and low expectations in their old schools as chief among their reasons for dropping out in the first place.

For many of the young people interviewed, inclusion of Romani language and history in the curriculum was important, as were visits from well-known Romani public figures. Support from teachers and exposure to role models were particularly important to students with less supportive parents. But principals and teachers seemed the most frustrated by the indifference of some parents. The students were more understanding. One young woman defended her mother: "Do not think that my mother is wicked and doesn't love us. She completed only three grades. She didn't have a positive experience of school and she doesn't know it is good for us."[27]

Regardless of the difficulties, most of the new Hungarian schools persist in bringing parents onto school premises regularly to persuade them that supporting their children's education now will bring future benefits.

For older students, economic pressures increase: many of those interviewed expressed a sense of responsibility to earn their keep and to help support their families. Students often had part-time jobs; and those who received scholarships with subsidies for travel, schoolbooks, and meals often gave part of their scholarships to their families. Any curriculum design must address the fact that many Roma students must work and study. The Hungarian models educate to a high standard, and their programs are demanding. Nevertheless, they accommodate their working students. Making it impossible for such students to earn some income would force students to make fateful choices—support their families as other family members do or pursue their own desires for individual advancement by attaining more education.

Not surprisingly, the new Hungarian Roma secondary school initiatives have higher dropout rates than the national average. Half of the Gandhi School's first intake of students dropped out, prompting a revision of the school's admissions policy and methodology. Still, half the class did graduate—a significant achievement—and the dropout rate declines year after year. Of the 18 students from the class of 2000, seven went to university, and 11 enrolled in vocational programs while planning to reapply for university admission the following year. Of the eight students at Collegium Martineum who completed their studies in 1999, five went on to higher education.

Second Chance Programs

Hungary and Romania have introduced initiatives that offer remedial and vocational training to students who lack secondary school diplomas. "Second Chance" programs target young people who have either dropped out of schools or whose personal circumstances put them at risk for dropping out. For example, the Don Bosco Primary and Vocational School in Hungary was originally established for a small number of young people placed under state guardianship. The Roma Chance Alternative Vocational School targets young people who have dropped out of school and offers hostel accommodations for students in need. In Romania, "Sec-

---

[27] Interview conducted for Save the Children (2001).

ond Chance" programs have been criticized for their narrow focus on a few low-status occupations such as car maintenance and metalwork. By way of contrast, neighboring Hungary has higher aspirations for its young Roma, evident in the wider opportunities offered there. But the young Romania Roma who availed themselves of the "Second Chance" training saw the opportunity to gain marketable skills, however lowly, as important.

In Romania, one cannot obtain a driver's license without completing compulsory education. For many young dropouts, a driver's license was an important incentive to re-enroll in, and complete, school.

Because statistics are not kept on the employment status of graduates, it is difficult to assess the effectiveness of these initiatives. Have the students progressed to employment, and, if they did, to what kind? We don't know. But the demand for these programs indicates that young Roma think the programs offer useful skills and opportunities. This is particularly true in Hungary, where, for example, at the Don Bosco school, Roma student numbers have increased from 30 in 1988 to more than 400 in 1999. In Romania, a review is under way, leading to a possible expansion of the "Second Chance" vocational programs.

The Integration-Segregation Debate

Critics of the Gandhi School's approach argue that it is another form of segregation: a "better class of ghetto." Not surprisingly, Roma leaders, educators, parents, and children themselves hold a range of views on the matter as to whether Romani students do better in settings designed specifically for a Roma context and in which students are protected from the racism and low expectations that they may encounter in schools with majority children.

There is no question that Roma, like other minorities, should be entitled to establish their own schools, if they so wish. Yet the motive, in many cases, for creating Roma model schools is the persistent failure of mainstream schools to adapt their curricula to the needs of minority students.

Roma-only model schools are preferred by traditional elements in Roma communities, which fear that an "education for all" ethic will divide families and destroy their unique cultural traditions. A recent UNDP survey shows, however, that most Romani parents prefer integrated school settings.

It is reasonable to conclude that the experience of successful model schools can be used elsewhere, to improve the performance of *all* schools. Most Romani parents appear to be comfortable with the prospect of their children attending alongside classmates from majority and other minority populations, provided their children are well-treated and supported in their transition to a mainstream curriculum.

The Debate over Mother-Tongue Instruction

Regarding the extent of demand for mother-tongue instruction (in this case, in the Romani language), debate continues. When surveyed, Roma parents continue to place low priority on mother-tongue instruction. They are instead more concerned that their children master the majority language well enough to learn in mainstream schools alongside majority children. Many parents take a pragmatic approach, differentiating between knowledge gained readily in the home and that which can be learned only in schools. Therefore, instruction in widely used European languages—such as English, French, and German—that can further a young person's employment prospects is seen as more desirable than mother-tongue instruction. The Romani language, like all minority languages, is important for family and cultural reasons; it is felt, with justice, that children should know enough to be able to converse with grandparents and members of their communities. However, schools are perceived to offer a different kind of education—an education that gives children skills and opportunities to get by in the wider world.

Nevertheless, activists are now arguing that instruction in Romanes has a symbolic importance over and above the utility of the subject. Inclusion in curricula would serve, activists argue, as a constant reminder to the majority population that Roma are citizens with histories, culture, and a language that merit study and respect. For young Roma in schools, a Romani studies course of study is an acknowledgement of their unique and therefore valuable ethnic identity. Once introduced, Romani language instruction is almost always popular with students. Roma students seen as less enthusiastic report they are sensitive about being singled out or because other children tease and insult them about attending so-called gypsy classes. In one Serbian school, for example, students were taunted about attending gypsy classes so they could learn to steal (Save the Children 2001). In this case, teachers were unwilling or unable to challenge racist bullying, and a well-intentioned curricular innovation backfired.

Gender Issues and "Adult Status" in Traditional Communities

European educational systems have perhaps the most difficult time accommodating one aspect of more traditional Romani communities: early betrothals and marriages. In Bulgaria a 1994 survey found that some 40 percent of Roma married before the age of 16, and 80 percent before the age of 18.[28] In traditional communities, it is not uncommon to withdraw Roma girls from school once they are 12 or 13 years of age, when families begin to look for potential husbands and arrange betrothals.

Coeducational schools during adolescence can therefore be viewed with suspicion. Male classmates are the means by which a young woman's reputation and thus her marriage prospects might be ruined. A relationship with a non-Romani, or with a Romani from a different community, could spell disaster for the entire family. In preparation for marriage, girls take on greater domestic and child-rearing duties. This apprentice adult status, in traditional Roma communities, also means Roma children become caregivers and wage earners years earlier than their peers in majority communities. Because the Romani culture does not always assign adult status to students, many older children, who desire adult status in the eyes of their community, drop out. This cultural norm explains in part the success Romania has had with its "Second Chance" programs discussed above. With their emphasis on practical and vocational skills (while including more academic elements from the high school curriculum), these program acknowledge that Roma students need their adult status to be validated.

Arranged (and sometimes forced) marriages, present challenges to the most culturally sensitive educators. On one hand, the point of educating girls should be

---

[28]Tomova (1998, 2000), cited in World Bank (2000).

empowering and even emancipating.[29] Yet any deep failures to accommodate traditional values reinforce the perception that the purpose of schools is to "deculture" Roma girls and teach them to defy their communities' rules. Experience in countries and communities with similar traditions suggests that successful approaches have worked *with*, rather than against, the culture, accommodating the community's norms as far as possible while finding ways to keep young women in education within the norms. Grade school education for this generation of girls, too, may translate into high school or even university for the next generation of Roma daughters.

Women working within traditional cultures to educate younger community members, including their own children, can be highly effective in achieving gradual change with the support of their communities. If girls are to stay in school, men and older women in the community must be assured that girls will not be put in situations that might compromise their honor or marriage prospects. Although segregating students is rarely a desirable option, separate facilities for the older girls may be a pragmatic solution if community elders are to consent to continued schooling—this accommodation might be made even more attractive if community elders were asked for their input on the curriculum.

Young women with family and childcare responsibilities, like their male counterparts who must work to help the family, need flexible hours and the option of bringing their children (or even an older women as a chaperone) with them when they attend courses. Husbands and mothers-in law are more likely to be supportive if the curriculum is seen to bring direct benefits to the family. If young Roma women are to continue their education, mainstream educators must respond with creativity, flexibility, and an open-mindedness.

Is Romani Culture Anti-Education?

It is common for some officials and teachers to blame Romani culture as the root cause of Roma enrollment, attendance, and performance deficits. The reality is more complex. Traditional Romani communities place a high emphasis on teaching their children to be good Romanies. Family and community are foremost: and the behaviors expected of young women and men, of wives, husbands, parents, and elders all have family and community at the center. Birth, betrothal, marriage, and death are significant life events solemnized with traditions and rituals. Learning these, and the language, history, music, and narrative they invoke, constitute an important part of a traditional Romani education. Children also learn practical skills that will help them to fulfill their adult roles: traditional crafts and trades, childcare, food preparation, and proper dress and demeanor.

So useful to family and community, these skills (and the knowledge they require) are readily apparent to the Roma. Less evident to many Roma parents is the utility of a formal education particularly against the educational legacy left by communist educational agendas in central and eastern Europe, which also, as it happens, relied almost completely on rote learning. Parents then rightly feared their children's values would be erased in the prevailing assimilationist climate. Although they generally accepted that basic reading, writing, and mathematics

---

[29] Young men, too, sometimes object to their families' choices of brides. The long-term consequences of defiance, however, are usually less harmful for young men.

were useful in the wider world, and saw value in vocational skills that might also bring in income, Roma parents perceived that few other aspects of the socialist curriculum had any relevance to Romani life.

As one study explains:

> After World War II, because governments used schools to enforce policies of assimilation, Roma were forcibly settled and expected to conform closely to rigid standards of sameness and display a demonstrative loyalty to the ethnic majority. Romani children were to learn such norms by having their "Romaniness" removed in school, and their culture itself was viewed as a package made up of social disadvantage and deviance that a tide of systematic schooling would cleanse (Cahn and others 1998).

Another oft-cited reason (indeed by Roma students themselves) for the antieducation bias seen among Roma parents is their own lack of formal education. Survey data gathered by UNDP for a recent report demonstrated that many Roma children lived in communities where few adults had completed even primary education. As a consequence, there are few adult Roma advocates for (formal) education beyond the most basic level. The UNDP survey found that in Bulgaria, 42 percent of Roma aged 15 or over had not completed even primary education. The corresponding figure for Romania was 47 percent. In both countries, just over 12 percent of adults had completed some kind of secondary education, usually vocational training.

The numbers of post-primary-age interviewees who had not completed even primary education were lower in the richer states, but still high: 34 percent in Hungary, 22 percent in Czech Republic, and 12 percent in Slovakia.

The recent UNDP study concluded, in part, that countries needed to take urgent action on the "ghetto mentality'" it saw as entrenched in the poorest Roma communities, where increasingly marginalized, impoverished, and socially isolated communities come to perceive that formal education is not for or about them. The report asserts that discrimination toward Roma children in schools often is a *reaction* to the visible manifestations of poverty, rather than a cause in itself. Teachers and non-Roma parents react atavistically to visible signs of poverty and ill health and seek to protect their healthy and well-presented children by shunning and segregating Roma children.

On their part, to protect their own and their children's self-esteem, Roma parents reject these institutions. It will take years, if not decades, to dismantle the pernicious legacy of so-called reduced curricula and special schools—a legacy that has so eroded the aspirations of Romani parents for their children and consigned tens of thousands of Romani children to a kind of educational apartheid. In the last decade, efforts to reform school governance, curricula, and teaching practice and to rebuild Romani parents' trust and confidence in the benefits of formal education have pointed out the direction reforms should take.

Concluding Remarks

Today, Roma activists and leaders are using the opportunities that have opened since 1990 and the prospect of EU accession to argue that joining a multinational, multiethnic, and multireligious club of rich nations makes educational reform a priority. Schools must teach children to acknowledge, accept, and respect diversity; and teachers must be prepared to work effectively with children from diverse backgrounds.

At the same time, Romani activists are advocating to their communities that formal education is increasingly essential—to enable their children to thrive in the modern economy. If they are to sustain their future families, children will need skills over and above those that the community can teach them. Furthermore, schools can be a means not only of self-improvement but also of strengthening pride in and knowledge of Romani identity.

Schools need Roma communities as a valuable local resource to help them meet the needs of an increasingly diverse student population. In turn, Roma communities need schools to help them to bring up young people who will be both "good Romanies" and good citizens of, and ambassadors to, a wider world.

Education alone cannot address the systemic factors that cause poverty, economic, and, ensuing social marginalization. But schools have an important role to play—diminishing social and cultural distances by building a sense of solidarity among children through the shared experience of learning not only about their own culture and identity but also the cultures and identities of their classmates. It is to be hoped that the "Decade of Roma Inclusion," and similar initiatives, will produce books and curricula on and about the history and culture of the Romani people, and that these will be available to *all* children. Only with these and other efforts can Europe begin, finally, to dismantle a centuries-old legacy that has blighted the life chances of so many thousands of children and young people.

References

Advisory Board (Advisory Board on Romani Affairs Finland). 1999. "Roma and Sinti Policies from Ideas to Implementation," paper submitted to the OSCE/Supplementary Human Dimension Meeting on Roma/Sinti Issues, September 6, 1999.

Cahn, Claude, David Chirico, Christina McDonald, Viktória Mohácsi, Tatjana Peric, and Agnes Székely. 1998. "Roma in the Educational Systems of Central and Eastern Europe." *Roma Rights* (Summer) 1998. Available from the European Roma Rights Center, http://www.errc.org.

Czech Helsinki Committee. 1997. *Report on the State of Human Rights in the Czech Republic.* See chapter 1, "Racism, Xenophobia, and the Position of Romanies." Czech Helsinki Committee, 1998. Available at http://www.helcom.cz/index_en .php > publications. Accessed May 2005.

Hancock, Ian. 2002. *We Are the Romani People.* Hatfield, Hertfordshire, England: University of Hertfordshire Press.

Khristo Kyuchukov, "Projects in Romani Education: Bulgaria." *Roma Rights* (Summer). Available from the European Roma Rights Center, http://www.errc.org.

Lavicka, Vojtech. 1998. "How Young Roma Live." *Roma Rights* (Summer). Available from the European Roma Rights Center, http://www.errc.org.

OSCE (Organization for Security and Co-operation in Europe). 2000. "Report and Recommendations on the Situation of Roma and Sinti in the OSCE Area." A recommendation of the High Commissioner on National Minorities. Vienna.

Available from http://www.osce.org/hcnm/ > documents. Accessed May 2005.

OSI (Open Society Institute). 2004. "OSI-NY Step By Step Roma Special Schools Initiative—Final Report." Available from http://www.osi.hu/esp/rei/research .html. Accessed May 2005.

Panayotova, Donka. 2002. "Successful Romani School Desegregation: The Vidin Case." *Roma Rights*, nos. 3–4. Available from the European Roma Rights Center, http://www.errc.org.

Save the Children. 2001. *Denied a Future? The Right to Education of Roma/Gypsy and Traveller Children.* 4 vols. Available from http://savethechildren.org.uk > resources > publications. Accessed May 2005.

Sobotka, Eva, and Sasa Uhlova. 1998. "Special Schools: Help or Harm for Romany Children?" http://www.czechia.com/hcaroma/newslett16.htm. Accessed May 2005.

Surdu, Mihai. 2002. "Quality of Education in Schools with a High Percentage of Roma Pupils in Romania." Paper prepared for the International Policy Fellowship Program, Open Society Institute, Budapest. A summary was published as "The Quality of Education in Romanian Schools with High Percentages of Romani Pupils," *Roma Rights*, nos. 3–4. Available from the European Roma Rights Center, http://www.errc.org.

UNDP. 2003. "Avoiding the Dependency Trap: The Roma in Central and Eastern Europe." Regional Human Development Report, New York.

Vassileva, Svetlana. 1998. "Things a Teacher Can't Forget." *Roma Rights* (Summer). Available from the European Roma Rights Center, http://www.errc.org.

World Bank. 2001. "Alternative Schools and Roma Education: A Review of Alternative Secondary School Models for the Education of Roma Children in Hungary." Working Paper 23027, Washington, DC. Available from http://www-wds.worldbank.org/.

6

Textbook Selection and Respect for Diversity in the United States

Susan Watts-Taffe

All students in public school classrooms have the right to materials and educational experiences that promote open inquiry, critical thinking, diversity of thought and expression, and respect for others. Denial or restriction of this right is an infringement of intellectual freedom.

—International Reading Association/
National Council of Teachers of English

In a multicultural, pluralistic society, the extent of democratic practices and the quality of democratic discourse hinge on citizens' orientations toward diversity.

—Avery and Hahn

The United States is one of the most diverse nations in the world. Its approximately 296 million people represent a wide range of ethnicities, native languages, religions, economic statuses, and political perspectives. Yet U.S. history is replete with institutional injustice. Large groups of people have been persecuted and murdered based on ethnicity, native language, gender, religious beliefs, sexual orientation, or for being poor. Today, the law protects such groups from persecution. Yet de facto racism and sexism continue, and numerous hate groups practice intolerance and violence against those deemed "different" (Southern Poverty Law Center 2003). It is in this context that public education is charged with engaging all children in, and preparing them for, critical thought, productivity, and the ability to fully participate in a pluralistic society (Hatcher 1979; Ladson-Billings 1994).

The importance of textbooks in the United States educational system cannot be overstated. Since the late 1800s, the vast majority of textbooks used in public schools has undergone some form of review and selection by a textbook adoption committee (Chambliss and Calfee 1998; Farr and Tulley 1985). Typically, the materials reviewed include student books and teachers' manuals. Thus, the textbooks selected may determine not only what but also how teachers teach and what and how students are expected to learn (Allington 2002; Chambliss and Calfee 1998; Jacob 2001). This chapter explores the status of textbook adoption practices in the United States, with particular emphasis on promoting respect for diversity.

Information gathered for this report was obtained primarily from three sources: (1) published literature on the topic; (2) descriptions of adoption policies and practices made available by state departments of education and local school districts, through written documentation, personal correspondence, and interviews; and (3) professional organizations, including the International Reading Association,

National Council of Teachers of English, National Council for the Social Studies, National Science Teachers Association, National Council of Teachers of Mathematics, and National Association of Multicultural Educators. The terms used to perform literature searches were "textbook adoption," "diversity," and "censorship."

In the review of documents pertaining to adoption procedures, and in interviews on this topic, I sought information on the overall adoption/selection process and on specific ways in which the process promotes respect for diversity. In-depth information was obtained for eight locales, representing five states, and a mix of urban, suburban, and rural school districts. Key personnel who either oversee or participate in textbook adoption processes in these districts were interviewed for anywhere from 20 minutes to one hour. Some interviewees answered additional questions via e-mail after the interview. The list of interview topics appears in box 6.1.

In this chapter, the term "textbook" is used primarily to refer to the books and teachers' manuals used to teach reading and language arts, social studies, science, and mathematics. It is used interchangeably with "instructional materials." "Selection" refers to the binding decision as to which texts to use with all students in a particular school, school district, or state. In the literature, "adoption" usually is used to refer to decisions made for entire states or large school districts. This term often involves the acceptance of multiple texts from which local districts or schools then make their final selections.

Findings

In this section, I describe my understanding of current textbook adoption practices in three parts. First, I outline the history of textbook adoption in the United States and briefly describe the current context within which textbook selection occurs. Second, I describe the adoption and selection processes followed in three areas of the country. Finally, I speak to the economics and politics of textbook selection.

Historical and Present-Day Contexts of Textbook Selection

Until the mid-1880s, a relatively small percentage of children received formal education. One-room schoolhouses served children of a wide range of ages, and schoolbooks consisted of whatever each child's parents could supply. When schooling

---

Box 6.1. Topics Addressed in Interviews about Adoption Processes

- Timeline for process and outline of activities
- Decision of which texts to consider
- Procedure for developing review committee(s)
- Demographic characteristics of a typical review committee
- Training for review committee(s)
- Timeline and procedure for review work
- Evaluation criteria and sheets
- Role of respect for diversity in evaluation criteria
- Role of respect for diversity in evaluation process
- Role of parent and/or citizen input in review process
- Final decisionmaking authority
- Existing adoption cycles

became available to more students, the single-class, mixed-textbook approach proved too cumbersome for teachers. It also proved inadequate in meeting the needs of so many students and so diverse a group of students. In addition, many parents did not have the money to purchase textbooks for their children.

In 1882 Massachusetts became the first state to mandate free textbooks for all students. Many states followed suit. Statewide adoption was created to provide uniformity in texts used by an increasingly mobile student population, to provide texts free of charge to all students, and to secure relatively low and uniform costs for textbooks across school districts in a state (Farr and Tulley 1985). The number of states that conduct what is known as "statewide adoption" has remained relatively unchanged since the early 1900s. There are 22 such states.

Of the 22 "adoption states," California, Texas, and Florida garner the most attention because they are the most populous. They account for a sizeable market share for any publishing company whose texts pass muster in those states (Chall and Squire 1991). In the remaining 28 nonadoption, or "open states," texts are selected at the level of the district or the individual school. In most large cities, texts are selected or adopted for the entire district. In open states, school districts may choose from among all textbooks on the market. Many school districts, in both adoption and open states, adopt new textbooks in five- to eight-year cycles (Chall and Squire 1991).

In adoption states, a state-level process is used to determine a list of texts that will be provided to students free of charge. Local districts, and individual schools in some cases, may select their texts from this approved list and have the cost covered by the state. Most states have a waiver policy by which a district may make an argument for purchasing a text not on the approved list. If the waiver is accepted, the state provides funds for the selection. If not, the district must provide its own funds for these texts.

It is helpful to think of statewide adoption as a two-tiered process in which a list of acceptable texts is determined by the state, based on review and evaluation (tier 1), followed by review and selection of a single text by local districts (tier 2). By contrast, open states have a one-tier process.

Historically, textbook selection practices have been criticized for several reasons, including inadequate or nonexistent training for those charged with making textbook recommendations, lack of or inadequate criteria for evaluation, lack of time devoted to the review process, and politics (Allington 2002; Erickson and Formalont 1979; Farr and Tulley 1985; Feynman 1999; Chall and Squire 1991; Jacob 2001; Stein and others 2001). Although textbook adoption processes are highly influential, they have not been extensively studied (Farr and Tulley 1985; Stein and others 2001).

Current Practices

In one of the most comprehensive studies of textbook adoption, Farr, Tulley, and Rayford (1987) noted a great deal of variation in approaches both between and within adoption and open states. Although there have been no recent studies of similar depth and breadth, the same appears true today (Chambliss and Calfee 1998). While it is difficult to point to one set of selection procedures as typical, there are, nonetheless, shared characteristics (Chall and Squire 1991; Chambliss and Calfee 1998; Farr and Tulley 1985; Stein and others 2001; Tyson-Bernstein 1988).

States employing statewide adoption share many common characteristics in their approaches to textbook selection. Compare, for example, the adoption policies of California (California Department of Education 2002), Florida (Florida Department of Education 2003), and Texas (Texas Education Agency 2003). Large urban districts tend to be similar to states in their adoption techniques. In both cases, adoption involves several layers of decisionmaking, much written policy, and the possibility that those responsible for making the critical decisions are removed from the actual use of the materials. In this regard, it is important to remember that some of the largest urban districts in the United States serve as many children as some of the smallest states. Small districts, often those in rural areas, tend to be much less bureaucratic in their textbook-selection procedures. Fewer people are involved in decisionmaking, and they are the individuals who actually will use the materials. Suburban districts seem to vary, with some being more similar to urban districts and others more similar to rural districts.

Centralized selection processes almost always involve a public presentation in which citizens can voice their opinion about the materials under consideration. Larger districts and states are more likely to work on a fixed adoption schedule than are smaller districts, which tend to engage in a selection process when they identify a need for new materials (Lohr 1979). Many adoption processes include opportunities to hear the opinions of a diverse group of individuals, although this opportunity is realized to varying degrees. For example, some procedures call for a deliberate effort to diversify the selection committee by gender and ethnicity. Other procedures include a separate review of materials by a person or group with expertise in multicultural education. Still other procedures rely on voluntary review by parents or other citizens presumed to provide diverse perspectives. In the remainder of this section, I consider an example from each of three locales: California, an urban district in the Midwest, and a rural district in the Northeast. Box 6.2 illustrates various steps of the adoption process as they occur in the three areas.

Statewide Adoption: California

In the state of California, an estimated 6 million children are affected by the kindergarten through eighth grade (K–8) statewide textbook-adoption process (U.S. Census Bureau 2002). Here the adoption process begins even before the textbooks have been written, with the publication of selection criteria at least 18 months prior to the time of adoption. These criteria include specifications regarding the physical durability of the text, the deadline for receiving submissions, and reference to the state curriculum and testing standards. A fixed adoption schedule ensures that the state and the publishers adhere to a predetermined timetable for requesting and submitting materials, respectively. The review process involves four groups: an instructional materials advisory panel/content review panel, legal and social compliance review panel, members of the public, and the curriculum commission (California State Board of Education 2002).

In a recent adoption of reading/language arts texts, the California instructional materials advisory panel and the content review panel consisted of 103 members, including classroom teachers, school administrators, local school board members, and parents/guardians. Members of the panels were appointed by the state board of education based on advice from the curriculum commission. Members of the panels are volunteers who are not compensated for their work. According to the

---

Box 6.2. *Three Processes for Adopting Textbooks*

Statewide adoption: California	*Local selection: Large urban district in Midwest*	*Local selection: Small rural district in Northeast*
• Invitation to submit • Development of evaluation criteria • Appointments to three review panels • Committee training • Review conducted by instructional materials advisory panel/ content review panel • Public review • Review conducted by legal and social compliance review panel • Recommendation to curriculum commission • Review and recommendation by curriculum commission • Decision by board of education (multiple texts) • Local review processes	• Chair's selection of materials to review • Appointment to two review panels • Development of evaluation rubric • Committee training/ orientation • Review conducted by evaluation committee • Review conducted by multicultural education specialist • Parent review • Recommendations to board of education • Decision by board of education (one text)	• Committee's selection of materials to review • Delegation of review to existing committee • Selection of evaluation criteria from publisher • Review conducted by evaluation committee • Piloting • Review of specific questionable selections by Native American Service Provider Committee • Recommendation to board of education • Decision by board of education (one text)

---

state board of education, the application process for participation on the panel is widely advertised. The goal is a panel that includes teachers from a range of districts—urban, suburban, and rural—who represent a range of K–8 grades, geographical regions in the state, and experiences. However, this seemingly open panel participation is limited to school districts that will provide the two weeks of release time so that their teachers can get the needed one week of training and one week of committee deliberation.

Generally, the instructional materials advisory panel is composed of those who work with children in the classroom and are concerned primarily with the usability of the text, whereas the content review panel consists of experts in the field, often university professors or practicing professionals, who review the materials for accuracy. In the recent reading/language arts adoption, these panels were trained together for one week during which they focused on the state's English-language arts content standards and reading/language arts framework, the board-approved evaluation criteria, and the adoption process. In addition, they heard presentations by publishers whose programs were under consideration. The very detailed evaluation criteria, described in 15 pages of single-spaced text, were divided into five categories:

(1) alignment with the content of the English-language arts content standards, (2) program organization, (3) assessment, (4) universal access, and (5) instructional planning and support.

Following training, committee members spent approximately two months conducting independent reviews of the materials. They then met for a week of group deliberation. The result of this deliberation was a report, written for each submitted textbook, which included a summary of the instructional materials, a recommendation, and reference to each of the five categories of the evaluation criteria. After these reports were written, the textbooks underwent a legal and social compliance review. Thirty-nine volunteers from around the state were selected to review the programs to ensure that they met standards for evaluating instructional materials for social content (California Department of Education 2001). These standards reflect the state education code and board of education policy. They also address the promotion of respect for diversity in instructional materials.

As panelists were being trained for their review process, textbooks under consideration were displayed at various centers throughout the state for public review and comment. At this time, citizens were invited to make written comments on the textbooks. Later in the process, before final actions were taken, public hearings were held.

Final recommendations were made by the curriculum commission; the final decision rested with the state board of education. At the end of the process, six textbook programs were adopted. Local school districts then conducted their own review processes to select textbooks from among these six. The timeline of the state adoption process was arranged to allow time for local school districts to pilot textbooks as part of their review process.

Local Selection in an Open State: An Urban District in the Midwest

In a large urban district in the Midwest, roughly 50,000 children are affected by textbook-adoption decisions. The 12–18 month process is coordinated by content-specific curriculum coordinators. In this district, there is no adoption schedule. Rather, new texts are considered when there is a felt need for new materials and the financial resources to purchase them. The review process consists of an evaluation conducted by the evaluation committee, which includes the multicultural education specialist. If there are questions about the content of materials with regard to multicultural perspectives, the materials are further reviewed by others in the district who specialize in reviewing materials for multicultural, gender-fair, disability-aware content.

In the most recent adoption of K–8 reading/language arts texts, the reading/language arts curriculum coordinator was responsible for making committee appointments, developing evaluation criteria, providing training, and chairing the committee (DeLapp 2003). She invited textbook submissions from all major and supplemental publishers listed in a directory of educational publishers. An open invitation was issued to teachers within the district to apply to participate on the evaluation committee. To get equal representation from each of five major geographical areas in the district as well as from the primary and intermediate grades, and to obtain a diverse committee with respect to gender and ethnicity, the chair actively recruited teachers and principals for committee membership. In addition, the committee included specialists in areas such as multicultural education, gifted-and-talented education, and the education of English-language learners. In all, the committee represented four ethnic groups, at least two religions, two sexual orientations, and two genders. The committee members' teaching experience ranged from 2 to 30 years. Teachers on the committee were paid for their time. Committee members with administrative classifications were not.

The chair developed a rubric for evaluating the textbooks and divided the task of evaluating materials among committee members, with three members reviewing each textbook under consideration. This rubric was heavily influenced by state and district grade-level expectations and standards. Guided by district policy, the committee used a separate checklist to assess the degree to which materials were multicultural, gender fair, and disability aware. The district multicultural specialist trained the committee members in this aspect of the evaluation. In addition, she personally reviewed materials from publishers that were not in use in the district as well as any materials that other members questioned.

After an initial round of reviews, some texts were eliminated. Publishers of the remaining texts were invited to give a presentation, which also was rated by committee members. After a second round of eliminations, the publishers whose materials still were in the running were invited to make a second presentation, which included a sample staff development session. All schools in the district were invited to send representatives to this presentation, and all representatives were given an opportunity to evaluate this aspect of the process. At this point, teacher teams visited school districts with similar demographics to see various programs that were using the potential selections in action. The district and the respective publishers shared the cost of these visits. Parental opinion was sought as well. These experiences led to the final recommendation made by the committee, which was acted on by superintendent and the board of education.

Local Selection in an Open State: A Rural District in the Northeast

In this school district, serving 1,500 students, textbook adoption does not occur in a regular cycle (Pascarella 2003). Furthermore, adoptions within a particular content area may be building-specific or grade-level-specific. The written protocol is sparse, and committees have quite a bit of latitude in determining their process. An intact committee, such as the K–12 curriculum committee or the science department, usually takes responsibility for the review process, with the involvement of at least one school principal. In a recent adoption of reading/language arts texts, publishers were invited to make presentations at the beginning of the process; the evaluation form used during the review process was theirs. Materials were reviewed during the time normally set aside for staff development. The entire process took approximately nine months, including more publisher presentations and a short period for piloting. Then a recommendation was made to the school board. Although not always the case, this particular committee represented the ethnic diversity of the community, which is 30 percent Native American. In addition, a Native American Service Provider Committee provided outside judgment on stories that featured Native American characters.

Economics and Politics of Textbook Selection

The publishing industry, textbook content, and selection procedures are intertwined. While publishers provide the supply from which adoption and selection committees must choose, states and large school districts provide the demand and, with it, the rules by which they decide what to purchase (Chambliss and Calfee 1999; Farr, Tulley, and Powell 1985). The strong influence that large adoption states such as California, Texas, and Florida have on textbook content and, therefore, on what is available nationwide, is widely documented (Berlak 1999; Honig 1991). The closed-door methods that are sometimes used, which override the hard work and inclusive voices represented by selection committees, also have been discussed in the literature (Ladson-Billings 1994; Jacob 1991). Other authors are more optimistic, suggesting ways that the processes of adoption and production can be used proactively to design the most effective curriculum and instruction for the nation's children (Chambliss and Calfee 1998). Indeed, Reutzel, Sudweeks, and Hollingsworth (1994) found that the majority of statewide textbook adoption committee members whom they surveyed felt that their work had a large, positive impact on the quality of reading and language arts programs in their states.

Promoting Respect for Diversity: Recommendations for Major Stages of the Selection Process

Clearly, U.S. textbook-selection processes have room for improvement. Still, what has evolved since the beginning of the twentieth century is a set of general procedures, from which lessons can be learned and for which recommendations can be made. The remainder of this section provides recommendations for the promotion of respect for diversity in the textbook-selection process, as related to major components of the process.

Composing the Evaluation Committee

Recommendation 1. Compose evaluation committees to include diverse perspectives, representative of the diversity in the community, subject-specific knowledge, and pedagogical knowledge.

Most of the work of evaluating textbooks is done by evaluation committees. In adoption states and in large school districts, there usually is an effort—at least a purported one—to compose a committee that is representative of the state or district as a whole, although it appears that committees often are homogeneous. Researchers have argued the importance of all individuals having the opportunity to participate in discussions related to the selection process (Erickson and Formalont 1979). Chambliss and Calfee (1998) suggest that ideal committee membership includes teachers who are knowledgeable in the subject-matter content and pedagogy, from diverse ethnic backgrounds, and educated and experienced in teaching a wide variety of students. Parent participation on the committee would represent the diversity within the student population.

Recommendation 2. Consider maintaining continuity from one adoption cycle to the next and providing some type of reward or payment for committee service.

The fact that selection committees generally do not make a deliberate effort to retain members from one adoption cycle to the next interferes with committee effectiveness. In addition, the volunteer status of the committee is not commensurate with what often is an overwhelming task. Providing payment for committee service might enhance the pool of teachers interested in participating and might increase the quality of their participation.

Developing the Evaluation Criteria

Recommendation 3. Include items related to respect for diversity in evaluation protocols.

Criteria for evaluation vary widely. Most school districts incorporate a uniform evaluation form, checklist, or rubric, while others allow evaluators to frame their evaluations entirely on their own. Most sets of criteria for evaluation focus on accuracy of content; scope, sequence, and pacing of content; usability for teachers; and alignment with state or district curriculum or testing benchmarks. Too often, attention to diversity is mentioned during the orientation process but is not included on the formal evaluation sheets, which are used to inform final recommendations and written reports.

Recommendation 4. Use evaluation tools that require more than a checkmark.

In some cases, evaluation forms are designed to require reviewers to comment or rate materials on quality. In others, reviewers are checking for the existence of certain characteristics rather than the quality of these characteristics. Forms also vary in level of detail. Some provide general guidelines left to the individual interpretation of committee members, while other forms are more specific. It is generally agreed that checklists promote only cursory attention to issues of quality (Tyson-Bernstein 1988). The more powerful tools require the reviewer to rate or write.

Recommendation 5. Test and revise evaluation tools before conducting the review.

To increase the probability that evaluation tools create the desired effect, it is important to test their use among reviewers. Those who coordinate the review process can accomplish this by having reviewers use the tools with selected materials, then engaging reviewers in a discussion of how they used the tools and what difficulties and ambiguities they encountered. Of course, this requires that adequate time be built into the review process to accommodate the development of strong evaluation tools.

Preparing/Training Evaluators

Recommendation 6. Provide committee members with adequate time to learn the review process and ample time to conduct their reviews.

Preparing the reviewers to evaluate textbooks effectively is critical. Yet, Tyson-Bernstein (1988) found that it is not uncommon for evaluation committee members to have no prior experience and receive no formal training. According to Muther (1986), training should not be limited to an orientation. It also should include a review of the latest research in the subject of study.

It is also imperative that sufficient time be provided for the review to enable reviewers to read and evaluate entire units of study. It is better for individual reviewers to evaluate small sections in depth and "planfully" than for reviewers, overwhelmed with the charge of reading several complete texts, to engage in the "flip test." Of course, the ideal is for individuals to read entire texts in a systematic manner.

Recommendation 7. Provide committee members with specific examples for each criterion, discussing both good and bad examples, and provide time for practice with the evaluation tools.

In their examination of 70 criteria sheets, Farr and Tulley found an average of 73 items per sheet, with equal weight given to all factors. With regard to each criterion, they state, "There is no discussion of what differentiates a good example from a bad one" (1985: 470). Committee members benefit from concrete examples of respect for diversity contrasted with examples of inaccuracy, disrespect, or intolerance.

Role of Frameworks and Standards

Recommendation 8. Build respect for diversity into frameworks and standards and in any bid specifications for publishers.

As previously indicated, state curriculum frameworks and standards play a central role in the evaluation of textbooks. In many states, such standards reflect those put forth by national professional organizations. For example, the National Council for the Social Studies (NCSS 1994) includes respect for diversity in several of its themes, including those of culture and global connections. In addition, standards one and nine of the Standards for the English Language Arts pertain specifically to respect for diversity (IRA/NCTE 1996). According to the National Association for Multicultural Education (NAME 2001):

> State curriculum standards designed to guide public education need to include the particular contributions, distinct heritages and values, as well as the multiple ways of knowing that represent our diverse population. Curricula should be designed to facilitate the development of individuals who appreciate the complexity of the human condition and who can effectively negotiate the diverse cultural contexts of U.S. society.

NAME has established curriculum guidelines corresponding to five areas of concern: inclusiveness, diverse perspectives, accommodating alternative epistemologies/social construction of knowledge, self-knowledge, and social justice.

Public Opinion and Piloting

Recommendation 9. Develop systematic methods of collecting public opinion and piloting textbooks under consideration.

Most school districts and states provide a forum for public response to textbooks that are under consideration. Those with the most persistent and organized voices have held greatest sway in selection proceedings, even when their opinions have not been representative of the larger community. Therefore, it is important to seek public opinion in ways that ensure representation from *all* constituencies. Likewise, piloting of textbooks should be done in an organized manner, with similar units of study tested across books and for a specified and equal period of time.

Designing and Reviewing the Selection Process

Recommendation 10. Invest time and resources in the careful design of selection procedures and include diverse voices in this process. Within this design, allow adequate time for each phase of the process and include a plan for regular, periodic review of the effectiveness of the process.

The first nine recommendations contribute to the overall design of the selection process. In this regard, Chambliss and Calfee (1998) make a clear distinction between "responders" and "designers." Responders tend to be superficial in their review of instructional materials. Less methodical and systematic than designers, they tend to react to what is on the market. Designers, on the other hand, attempt to shape the market. By using well-planned, thorough selection processes based on a strong sense of what they want, designers help drive the production of texts to meet their needs. The school districts that report the greatest satisfaction with their selection processes are those whose procedures were well planned and reflect current thinking in the areas of curriculum and instruction. By revisiting the process on a regular basis, educators open themselves to continuous growth related to promoting respect for diversity.

Final Thoughts and Suggestions for Further Research

An in-depth look at textbook adoption practices and policy brings forth several important issues. One such issue is the relation between textbook adoption and pedagogy (Farr and Tulley 1985). First, the textbooks adopted play a significant role in shaping teachers' understandings of what it is that they are teaching and of effective teaching practice. Second, school districts increasingly are relying on textbook publishers to provide staff development for their teachers.

A recurring theme in articles that question the effectiveness of current textbook-adoption practice is that of critical thinking versus rote memorization, and higher-order thinking versus basic skills. Several writers note that the more discrete and controlling the curriculum frameworks and standards for a state or a district—and thus the more textbook publishers work to create books that meet such discrete skills—the less cohesive the texts are as a whole, the less engaging, and the less motivating. There are two important points here. First, critical thinking would seem to be paramount to the acceptance, encouragement, and presentation of multiple social perspectives. Second, poorly written books may have the most detrimental effect on those students most reliant on public schooling and textbook content for their intellectual growth.

We all are aware of the respect-for-diversity mirage. With regard to textbook content, there are numerous examples of the peripheral treatment of "diverse groups" in lieu of the true integration of diverse perspectives (Cornbleth and Waugh 1999). Certainly, the selection process is not immune to such surface-level approaches. Yet, the dearth of research on textbook adoption, both generally and specifically related to issues of diversity, is striking. Clearly, there is a need for research in this area, with particular attention to promoting respect for diversity as it occurs in both policy and practice.

References

Allington, R. L. 2002. *Big Brother and the National Reading Curriculum: How Ideology Trumped Evidence*. Portsmouth, NH: Heinemann.

Avery, P. G., and C. Hahn. 2004. "Diversity and U.S. 14-Year-Olds' Knowledge, Attitudes, and Experiences." In *Education Programs for Improving Intergroup*

Relations Programs, ed. W. G. Stephan and W. P. Vogt (380–405). New York: Teachers College Press.

Berlak, H. 1999. "Standards and the Control of Knowledge." *Rethinking Schools Online* 13(3). http://www.rethinkingschools.org/archive/13_03/control.shtml. Accessed June 2005.

California Department of Education. 2001. *Standards for Evaluating Instructional Materials for Social Content*. Sacramento: California Department of Education.

California State Board of Education. 2002. "2002 Reading/Language Arts/English Language Development (RLA/ELD)." http://www.cde.ca.gov/ci/rl/im/. Accessed June 2005.

Chall, J. S., and J. R. Squire. 1991. "The Publishing Industry and Textbooks." In *Handbook of Reading Research*, ed. R. Barr, M. L. Kamil, P. Mosenthal, and P. D. Pearson, vol. 2 (120–46). White Plains, NY: Longman.

Chambliss, M. J., and R. C. Calfee. 1998. *Textbooks for Learning: Nurturing Children's Minds*. Malden, MA: Blackwell.

Cornbleth, C., and D. Waugh. 1999. *The Great Speckled Bird: Multicultural Politics and Education Policymaking*. Mahwah, NJ: Erlbaum.

DeLapp, P. 2003. Personal correspondence. March 5.

Erickson, L. G., and M. M. Formalont. 1979. "Criteria for the Evaluation of Reading Materials." In *Indoctrinate or Educate?* ed. T. C. Hatcher and L. G. Erickson (48–50). Newark, DE: International Reading Association.

Farr, R., and M. A. Tulley. 1985. "Do Adoption Committees Perpetuate Mediocre Textbooks?" *Phi Delta Kappan* 66: 467–71.

Farr, R., M. A. Tulley, and P. Powell. 1987. "The Evaluation and Selection of Basal Readers." *The Elementary School Journal* 87(3): 267–81.

Farr, R., M. A. Tulley, and L. Rayford. 1987. "Selecting Basal Readers: A Comparison of School Districts in Adoption and Non-Adoption State." *Journal of Research and Development in Education* 20(4): 59–72.

Feynman, R. P. 1999. "Judging Books by Their Covers." *The Textbook Letter, 1–9.* July-August. http://www.textbookleague.org/103feyn.htm. Accessed June 2005.

Florida Department of Education. 2003. Instructional Materials and Library Media. http://www.firn.edu/doe/instmat/home0015.htm. Accessed June 2005.

Hatcher, T. C. 1979. "Educational Directions in a Pluralistic Society." In *Indoctrinate or Educate?* ed. T. C. Hatcher and L. G. Erickson (38–41). Newark, DE: International Reading Association.

Honig, B. 1991. "California's Experience with Textbook Improvement." In *Textbooks in American Society: Politics, Policy, and Pedagogy*, ed. P. G. Altbach (106–16). Albany, NY: SUNY Press.

Jacob, B. 2001. "Implementing Standards: The California Mathematics Textbook Debacle." *Phi Delta Kappan* 83: 264–72.

Ladson-Billings, G. 1994. "Whose Schools Are They Anyway? The Quest for Democratic and Equitable Education." *Social Studies Review* 33(2): 6–11.

Lohr, E. 1979. "Materials Selection Processes: Why and How?" In *Indoctrinate or Educate?* ed. T. C. Hatcher and L. G. Erickson (51–56). Newark, DE: International Reading Association.

IRA/NCTE (International Reading Association/National Council of Teachers of English). 1996. *Standards for the English Language Arts*. Newark, DE: International Reading Association.

Muther, J. 1986. "What 'Training' Should Be Provided?" *Educational Leadership* 43: 84–85.

National Association for Multicultural Education. 2001. "Criteria for Evaluating State Curriculum Standards." http://www.nameorg.org/resolutions/state-curr.html. Accessed June 2005.

NCSS (National Council for the Social Studies). 1994. Curriculum Standards for Social Studies: Executive Summary. http://www.socialstudies.org/standards/execsummary/. Accessed June 2005.

Pascarella, J. 2003. Personal correspondence. March 12.

Reutzel, D. R., R. Sudweeks, and P. M. Hollingsworth. 1994. "Issues in Reading Instruction: The Views and Information Sources of State-Level Textbook Adoption Committee Members." *Reading Research and Instruction* 34: 149–71.

Ross, E. P. 1989. "A Model for Basal Reader Adoption." Paper presented at the meeting of the International Reading Association, New Orleans, LA. May.

Southern Poverty Law Center. 2003. "Active Hate Groups in the United States in 2000." No longer available online. But see "The Year in Hate" at http://www.splcenter.org/intel/intelreport/article.jsp?aid=233. Accessed June 2005.

Stein, M., C. Stuen, D. Carnine, and R. M. Long. 2001. "Textbook Evaluation and Adoption Practices." *Reading and Writing Quarterly* 17(1): 5–28.

Texas Education Agency. 2003. "Textbook Administration." http://www.tea.state.tx.us/textbooks/. Accessed March 2003 and June 2005.

Tyson-Bernstein, H. 1988. *A Conspiracy of Good Intentions: America's Textbook Fiasco*. Washington, DC: Council for Basic Education.

U.S. Census Bureau. 2002. "State and County Quick Facts." http://quickfacts/census.gov/qfd/states/0600.html. Accessed March 2003.

Part III
Applications

7

Social Analysis in the Design of World Bank Education Projects

Ian Bannon

Educational assistance projects carried out in deeply divided societies will be more successful if designed in light of a formal *social analysis* that examines the fault lines and stress points that may compromise social cohesion. In countries that are in conflict, emerging from conflict, or vulnerable to an eruption of widespread violence, a successful intervention will likely require specialized analyses of the conflict and of the role of the education system in exacerbating or attenuating it. These issues are illustrated in this chapter with reference to the role of education in Sri Lanka.

The chapter is based on several sources:

- *Reshaping the Future: Education and Post-Conflict Reconstruction,* by the World Bank's Human Development Network Education Hub (Buckland 2004)
- Recent work on incorporating social dimensions in Bank-supported projects (World Bank 2003b)
- Social analysis guidelines for the education sector under preparation by the Social Analysis and Policy Group in the Bank's Social Development Department (World Bank 2004), as well as earlier work by the Conflict Prevention and Reconstruction unit of the Social Development Department (World Bank 2002).

World Bank Lending for Education

Investing in education plays a key role in meeting the World Bank's social development objectives, which support inclusion, social cohesion, and accountability in development. Since 1963, when it made its first education loan for vocational training in Tunisia, the Bank has greatly expanded its education portfolio. It is now the single largest external source of finance for education in the developing world. During the past 35 years, the World Bank has loaned $30 billion to support 675 education projects in more than 120 countries. Over the past five years, annual Bank lending for education has averaged $1.6 billion.

An early concentration on building schools and providing equipment has given way to greater focus on quality and content, with an emphasis on primary education. Today almost 50 percent of the World Bank's education lending goes to training, technical assistance, textbooks, and sectoral reforms. The Bank works with its client countries to improve access for those previously excluded from education, particularly girls, the rural poor, and linguistic or other excluded minorities. It is reaching out to the 900 million illiterate adults in the developing world, two-thirds of whom are women, to bring education into villages and homes, in some cases through distance learning. These efforts reflect the realization that projects and interventions that foster inclusion and social cohesion are likely to be more sustainable than other projects and to reach a larger number of beneficiaries.

For countries emerging from violent conflict, Bank support to rebuild ravaged education systems is often one of the earliest activities in postconflict reconstruction. Beyond simply restarting the preconflict education system, the Bank and other agencies that support postconflict reconstruction now emphasize the need for transformative approaches that will help societies become more inclusive and pluralistic and therefore less likely to fall back into violent conflict. Understanding the role of education systems in fostering greater social diversity, inclusion, and resilience to conflict has become an important element in the Bank's social development agenda.

By focusing on the opportunities and constraints facing different social groups, social analysis can maximize the positive impact of reforms and projects intended to increase access to education, and its quality, particularly for poor and vulnerable groups. Systematic social assessment goes a step further, strengthening participatory processes and building beneficiaries' sense of ownership of the project and its outcomes.

Why Social Analysis?

Social analysis improves project quality and sustainability by exposing the interplay between people and institutions. It traces barriers to opportunity, taking into account institutionalized rules of economic relations, categories of social diversity, and the interests and influence of multiple stakeholders in the project. Done well, it identifies social and institutional constraints and opportunities that may not be immediately apparent but that may influence project or policy objectives. Social analysis thus helps ensure that objectives are clear and achievable and that unintended consequences are avoided. Countries that are in, or at risk of, violent conflict call for more specific and targeted analyses. As described later in this chapter, where violent conflict is present or likely, conflict analysis is suggested as a specialized subset of broader social analysis.

Among the obstacles to equity and access that may come to light in a social analysis are:

- Forms of marginalization and discrimination
- The burden that poor or marginalized households may face from informal payments and school maintenance costs
- Problems in obtaining textbooks, school supplies, and school clothing[1]
- The link between school attendance and how beneficiaries perceive educational quality and relevance.

---

[1] In countries such as Armenia, Georgia, or Latvia, clothing often serves as a symbol of the parents' ability to provide for their children. Parents feel strong social pressure to provide a new outfit for the first day of school. Children (in the cities and villages) are involved in an expensive competition over clothes. They are aware of socioeconomic differences symbolized by clothing and feel deep shame if they are wearing old or shabby clothes when other children are well dressed (Social Development Department 2004).

Social groups can differ widely both in their interests and in their ability to advance those interests. Groups that lack the opportunity or the power to express their interests are often poor and vulnerable. Unless special efforts are made to understand and accommodate the interests of the poor, the cycle of poverty and powerlessness is likely to continue (World Bank 2001).

Social analysis complements traditional technical approaches to education by focusing on the *demand side* of education—the needs, interests, opportunities, voices, and potential of targeted beneficiaries. A purely technical approach might assume that, other things being equal, the benefits of a given project or reform will be more or less equitably distributed among beneficiaries. The unit of analysis in such approaches is usually the individual or the household, with relatively little focus on relationships among the units of analysis.

The social analysis perspective assumes the opposite: that benefits will *not* be equitably distributed precisely because different groups have unequal access, assets, and voice. In social analysis, the unit of analysis is the social group or category, and the interest is in relationships among these groups. Social analysis can make an important contribution to understanding demand-side constraints on education access, especially when poor and marginalized groups may not consider that public education is relevant or appropriate to their sociocultural realities and aspirations.

If an educational assistance project is to promote inclusivity and check the cycle of poverty, its design must reflect an understanding of the differences that separate groups and provide the means to bridge them, if only in school. For gains made in school generate ripple effects for many years. Access to education widens job and income opportunities for disadvantaged groups—girls and women, ethnic and linguistic minorities, the disabled, and isolated rural populations. For ethnic minorities, education makes possible economic and political participation. Educated minorities tend to be more active, articulate, and influential citizens. Conversely, poorly planned education systems can widen inequalities among socioeconomic, gender, and ethnic groups. Poor planning can limit the access of disadvantaged groups to quality education.

Social analysis helps the Bank and its clients anticipate and avoid unintended negative consequences of interventions such as school rationalization or consolidation. For example, children living in isolated rural communities may have less access to school following school rationalization if transport is poor or travel unsafe, or if local norms discourage children, particularly girls, from traveling unattended to school. To take another example, curriculum reform may entail difficult choices about the language of instruction. Depending on the politics of the reform, it may neglect indigenous concerns or reaffirm negative stereotypes of certain social groups (whether defined by ethnicity, disability, or gender). Reforms that call for increasing teacher qualifications may increase teachers' insecurity. In some cases, education authorities may use recertification examinations in an arbitrary manner to discriminate among certain groups of teachers. Or reforms may be unrealistic in assuming the existence of resources that are not available or have yet to be developed. The bilingual education program implemented in Nicaragua in 1994, for example, called for bilingual education for all ethnic groups until grade 6. However, the program was immediately confronted with a lack of bilingual teachers (World Bank 2004).

Social analysis can increase the effectiveness and impact of education projects in a variety of ways. Here are some examples.

- Education can be tailored to local values, particularly for indigenous communities or minorities whose norms and behaviors may differ significantly from those of the surrounding majority. For example, the *Indonesia Book and Reading Development Project* responded to large differences among regions and groups by allowing Provincial Education Services to select book series for each subject. The provincial offices could base their choices on local content, relevance, and local experience (World Bank 2004).
- Careful attention to the language of instruction and to implicit or explicit ethnic stereotypes and negative historical depictions of minorities can improve ethnic relations. Conversely, negative stereotypes or neglect of minorities and their languages can reinforce exclusionary practices, affirm popular prejudices, and contribute to violence and, ultimately, the eruption of conflict.
- Properly designed education programs can provide opportunities for constructive engagement to isolated, impoverished, or marginalized youths, who otherwise have few alternatives to alcohol, drugs, and violence. Such programs can be formal or informal, and can offer instruction, entertainment, or simply situations in which to improve social skills.
- Reform of education systems should be a part of a wider effort to increase transparency and accountability in government and institutional responsiveness to local constituencies. Schools and education are often a rallying point for communities. Encouraging meaningful engagement of teachers and parents is thus a good way to encourage demands for greater government accountability and increased ownership of reforms. In many developing countries, greater local involvement in education complements the general move toward decentralization and greater community empowerment. For example, El Salvador, India, and Nicaragua have found that devolving more autonomy to schools provides incentives for school personnel, parents, and community members to contribute actively to school affairs. When parents and community members formally participate in school councils and management, they put greater accountability pressures on schools, resulting in reduced teacher absenteeism (King and Ozler 1998).
- New technologies and forms of distance learning provide rural and other isolated populations with access to education. They offer ways to integrate these often poor populations into the national and global economy and to increase social integration among far-flung communities with little contact among themselves or with urban capitals. When appropriately designed, these new technologies may also offer opportunities for divided communities or groups to interact and build trust in a neutral and less confrontational space.

Doing Social Analysis

Bank social scientists use five entry points, or dimensions of inquiry, to structure their analyses (World Bank 2003b):

- Social diversity and gender
- Institutions, rules, and behavior

- Stakeholders
- Participation
- Social risk.

Depending on the country circumstances and the sectoral context, social analysis may be restricted or expanded, and some entry points may be more prominent than others.

Social Diversity

The Bank's framework for social analysis considers the assets, capabilities, social capital, and livelihoods of disadvantaged groups in the society that will host the project or program for which the social analysis is being conducted. It also considers the power relationships among different social groups. Such groups may be defined by gender, ethnicity, language, religion, cultural, spatial, economic, or other characteristics. In the education sector, ethnicity (often related to religion, language, or other identity markers), gender, and region are often associated with differential access to education and varying levels of educational quality and effectiveness.

It is important to consider how diversity is represented in the content of teaching, in the choice of language of instruction, in the modes and content of teacher training, in pedagogical practice, and in the stereotypes that textbooks and reading materials convey, explicitly and implicitly. By asking probing questions, social analysis helps us understand whether curricula, teaching materials, and teacher training reflect the values, outlook, history, and practices of all groups in the community.

- How do differences in gender, ethnicity, caste, spatial segregation, and economic status affect access to education and educational outcomes in the project area?
- How could the project contribute to improved opportunities for poor or socially excluded groups?
- What attitudes do various groups hold about the value of education in general and for girls and women in particular? How do these values and attitudes reflect and affect access to education and the project's objectives?
- Are there differences in enrollment, attendance, and outcomes (such as completion rates, access to tertiary education, access to the job market) among ethnic or linguistic groups, or between urban and rural populations? What are the patterns of inter-ethnic relations in the community and society? How integrated are ethnic groups in their local communities and society as a whole?

Ethnic, religious, and linguistic diversity can have an important bearing on educational achievement. For example, the values and practices of ethnic or religious minorities may bring them into conflict with the formal education system. Ethnic prejudice may encourage schools to stereotype children, who in turn underachieve and drop out. Such stereotyping may even lead administrators to "diagnose" minority children as mentally defective and exclude them from mainstream educational institutions. In parts of Eastern and Central Europe, these children have been sent to special schools, sometimes in residential institutions that offer limited, and now sorely underfunded, education (World Bank 2004). This practice is widespread in the case of Roma children in Eastern Europe (see chapter 5 in this volume).

Language policies also can have significant unintended consequences. Countries with diverse ethno-linguistic populations may insist on using textbooks in a single official language, in the belief that a single language and national curriculum are essential for national unity. When a significant portion of the national population does not speak the official language, however, such a policy can breed resentment rather than unity. Linguistic minorities may be further disadvantaged because their children cannot learn as quickly as other students. And language barriers may deter parents from becoming involved in the school system.

At their worst, ethnic cleavages feed social tension and violence, which can escalate into widespread conflict. Social analysis must explore dormant as well as overt conflicts among different social groups and expose the role of stereotyping in perpetuating them. In Albania, for example, urban-rural and socioeconomic differences have created serious tensions between rural migrants from the isolated and impoverished northeast and children from urban families (World Bank 2004). These tensions sometimes manifest themselves in physical violence, leading some rural children to drop out of school. High levels of street violence, and the violence characteristic of postconflict countries, interfere with education and affect the mental and physical health of children, encouraging many families to keep their children, especially girls, at home. In some countries, violent conflict results in the recruitment of children or teenagers to join the fighting forces.

Social cleavages are often layered, forming a web of social interactions that may interact in complex ways with state structures. Consider the Indian state of Uttar Pradesh, the nation's largest and one of its poorest. Uttar Pradesh's 160 million people must contend with poorly equipped and often distant schools, with teachers from different ethnic and language groups, and with school administrators from different socioeconomic backgrounds. Many poor families are skeptical of the value of education, particularly for girls. The state must also attempt to include disadvantaged groups, such as Muslims, lower-caste children, and working children, in the school system. Social analysis must be cognizant of these cross-cutting divisions and their likely effects on a project.[2]

Institutions, Rules, and Behavior

The focus of social analysis of institutions and organizations in the education sector is the political and socioeconomic aspects of education provision. In most countries a wide range of institutions provides education services, including government ministries (of education, labor, and social protection), the private sector, NGOs, and faith-based organizations. Social analysis can begin by mapping the range of involved institutions and organizations, their roles and responsibilities, their prevailing attitudes, their formal and informal rules and behaviors, and they way in which they affect service provision. Some questions to consider include:

- How transparent are education organizations and institutions, especially in terms of resource allocations, transfers, and staffing?

---

[2] The low literacy rates in India are compounded by enormous inequalities in terms of region, urban and rural population, gender, and social groups such as scheduled castes, scheduled tribes, and minorities.

- What is the role of nongovernment providers of education, and what formal and informal rules govern them?
- How are education decisions made at the central, regional, district, and school levels?
- How do involved institutions and organizations relate to civil society? Does the government see civil society organizations as partners or as undermining state authority?
- Where do lines of accountability point—toward central authorities, communities, parents, or other groups? What scope do parents have to affect the formal education of their children?

Stakeholder Analysis

Stakeholder analysis is a subset of the diversity analysis, focusing on the groups that are directly affected by, or can affect, a proposed project or policy. As in the society at large, considerable variation may exist within stakeholder groups—for example, between urban and rural areas, poor and rich neighborhoods, or different ethnic or linguistic groups. Stakeholder analysis normally asks the following questions:

- Which groups suffer from deficiencies in the education system, which groups benefit disproportionately from the system, and what does each group stand to gain or lose from the project in terms of access, responsibility, control, or income?
- Which groups are likely to oppose or undermine the project?
- Do intended beneficiaries give high priority to project benefits?
- If additional user costs seem necessary, will the benefits be tangible enough to warrant them, and will they affect groups differentially?
- What are the real and perceived needs and concerns of different stakeholders, such as access to educational opportunities and the quality of service?
- How do stakeholders express their needs and concerns? What coping mechanisms do they employ to overcome poor access, quality, or service?
- How do these coping mechanisms help or hinder attitudinal, behavioral, or other changes that the project seeks to foster?
- How are key stakeholders related to each other, and how may project activities change these relationships and social dynamics?
- What mediation and feedback mechanisms can the project use to reconcile diverse and conflicting views?
- Which key groups should be educated about the project, and what messages should be sent?

Stakeholder analysis can help sustain support for and reduce opposition to a project. It should produce practical guidelines for ensuring that stakeholders who are normally excluded from decisionmaking participate in project design and implementation.

Participation

Participation is a process through which stakeholders influence and share control over development initiatives and the decisions and resources that affect them. Project leaders and client governments solicit and encourage stakeholders' participation through consultations. Social analysis of participation looks at the mechanisms through which different stakeholders participate in the project, as well as the conditions that encourage or hinder the design of participatory processes.

The project's consultation and participation processes should be clearly linked with the stakeholder analysis. The process should ensure that key stakeholder groups are involved in the project and that expected benefits and outcomes are disaggregated among key groups so as to be perceptible to each group. Benchmarks, indicators, and monitoring and evaluation systems should proceed from and be consistent with the stakeholder analysis.

The nature of participation in education projects varies by context. In terms of service provision, participation may refer to engaging professionals inside government, including staff at different levels within the ministry of education and at the national, regional, and local levels. Shaping education policy and designing curricula also involve consultation among, and the participation of, government and civil society organizations such as academic institutions, teachers' unions, and faith-based, and community groups. Analysts should identify existing and potential mechanisms through which government officials and nongovernmental stakeholders at various levels can participate in implementation of the project. Community involvement is especially important, because it ensures diversity and inclusion.

- Community and parental involvement can help shape curricula and learning materials that reflect children's everyday lives and sociocultural realities.
- Communities can contribute to more inclusive schools by sending respected community members, such as religious or tribal leaders, to the classrooms to talk about community history, traditions, customs, and culture celebrated in the community.
- Project interventions that explicitly support community and parental participation in education can create an environment in which parents feel empowered to participate in schools.[3]

The Serbia Education Improvement Project, for example, encourages local communities to participate more effectively in education. Stakeholders, including ministry officials at all levels, school principals, teachers, parents, students, and their communities, identify local mechanisms through which to spend school funds. They also participate on school boards and sit on committees responsible for designing funding formulas to ensure equitable impact on minorities and disadvantaged groups (World Bank 2004).

Some key questions in assessing participation in education projects include:

- What mechanisms exist to ensure participation by groups that previously may have been excluded—among them women, the poor, and ethnic, religious, and linguistic minorities? If these groups lack the skills to participate meaningfully in different aspects of the project—for example, in school

---

[3]Many groups, especially minorities in developing countries, develop a negative attitude toward schools. Parents who do not speak the country's official language and embrace other than mainstream traditions and culture often feel discouraged in classrooms in which teachers do not show respect for their linguistic and cultural diversity. As a result, such parents may conclude that they are incapable of taking responsibility in school issues and that education is the exclusive domain of educational professionals (Uemura 1999).

management—does the project include a realistic and well-targeted capacity-building component? Are there other impediments to their participation, such as problems of transportation or scheduling?

- How can communities participate in designing funding mechanisms to ensure equity for minorities and the disadvantaged? How can participation be adapted to take into account the different needs and constraints of excluded and marginalized groups?

Social Risks

The social analysis of risks includes consideration of the sociocultural and political risks to the project or to reforms, as well as risks to society or to particular groups as a result of the intervention. Examination of social risks should begin with a clear understanding of how the project or initiative started and which stakeholder groups have been key in supporting or opposing the project or reforms.

Vulnerability risks. Will the project increase the vulnerability of any groups or communities? Particularly for the very poor and marginalized, education reform must consider ways to reduce the opportunity costs of enrolling children in school. Projects calling for mainstreaming children with social or physical disadvantages may actually increase these children's vulnerability to discrimination or exclusion, unless special efforts are made to sensitize education providers and provide the necessary support.

Political economy risks. Efforts to empower different groups may create new imbalances among stakeholders or marginalize one segment within a given stakeholder group. If the political elite belong to a linguistically distinct group, they may oppose institutionalizing linguistic diversity in schools, thus causing access barriers to those speaking a different language. Projects that try to address this problem may face resistance from the political establishment and elites. For example, as parent-teacher councils take on greater roles in managing schools, there is a danger that more prosperous and better-connected parents will dominate decisionmaking to the detriment of poorer families.

The World Bank's Conflict Analysis Framework

To address issues related to conflict and development, the Bank's Operational Policy on Development Cooperation and Conflict (OP2.30) calls for the integration of sensitivity to conflict in Bank assistance through conflict analysis (World Bank 2003a). The need for conflict analysis is based on the recognition that the probability of success of development assistance is improved by identifying sources of violent conflicts and opportunities for their outbreak and escalation. A better understanding of the sources and dynamics of conflict can help project and country teams ensure that interventions do not instigate, exacerbate, or revive situations of violent conflict, but instead—if well designed—reduce or mitigate it.

The Conflict Analysis Framework (CAF) developed by the Bank's Conflict Prevention and Reconstruction Unit (World Bank 2002) focuses on six areas:

- Social and ethnic relations
- Governance and political institutions
- Human rights and security

- Economic structure and performance
- Environment and natural resources
- External factors.

It also identifies four characteristics of a society that is resilient to violent conflict:

- Political and social institutions that are inclusive, equitable, and accountable
- Economic, social, and ethnic diversity rather than polarization and dominance
- Growth and development that provide equitable benefits across society
- A culture of dialogue rather than violence.

To ascertain whether a country needs to undertake conflict analysis, the CAF includes nine risk screening indicators, including ethnic dominance and youth unemployment.[4] High scores in several of these risk areas suggest the need for a full conflict analysis, covering six categories related to conflict. Each category contains several variables, each with corresponding levels of intensity that reflect changes in the level of violent conflict. The variables highlight sensitive issues that need to be taken into account in strategy or project design.

The key category for social development, and the one most relevant to the education sector, is social and ethnic relations.[5] The category is broken into eight variables: social and economic cleavages, ethnic cleavages, regional imbalances, differential social opportunities, bridging/bonding social capital, group identity-building, myth-building, and culture or tradition of violence.

The educational system is affected by and can influence each of these characteristics. Just as education has the potential to fan violent conflict, it also has the potential to instill new values, attitudes, skills, and behaviors, as well as promote new social relations that will build resilience to conflict.

The remainder of this chapter illustrates how, if the CAF had been applied to Sri Lanka before the conflict escalated (in the late 1960s and early 1970s) and at various points as the conflict evolved, policymakers and development partners could have focused on the role of education policies in triggering and escalating the conflict between the government and the Tamil rebel movement. It starts with a brief background to the conflict and ends with the policy implications that might have emerged from the application of the CAF.

An Opportunity Missed: The Case of Sri Lanka

Conflicts have plagued Sri Lanka since its independence in 1948. In addition to the long-running war between the Liberation Tamil Tigers of Eelam (LTTE) and the Sinhalese-dominated government, the country has seen intra-Tamil warfare for political control; intermittent clashes between the Tamils and Muslims, particularly in the East, where Muslims speak Tamil but generally support the government; and sporadic insurrections against the government by the Janatha Vimukthi Peramuna, a radical, rural-based Sinhalese youth movement.

---

[4]The other indicators are history of conflict, income per capita, primary commodity exports, political instability, political and civil rights, militarization, and active regional conflicts.
[5]The other categories of variables include governance and political institutions, human rights and security, economic structure and performance, environment and natural resources, and external factors (World Bank 2002).

Sri Lanka is inhabited by the majority Sinhalese and minority Tamils, plus a relative small number of Muslims. The Sinhalese and Tamils both claim that they have always been separate, ethnically defined nations and were the first "colonizers" of the island. They tend to overlook two important facts. First, the two groups of invaders—the Sinhalese from the north of India and the Tamils from the South—intermingled with each other and with the autochthonous people they found on the island when they arrived.[6] By the time of Ceylon's independence, the Tamils were concentrated in the north and in the Sinhalese in the south and southwest, with Sinhalese and Tamils mixing on the eastern part of the island. The two groups developed separate identities, customs, and traditions, but viewed each other positively and lived in considerable harmony in the east.

The cooperation that marked relations between the English-speaking Tamil and Sinhalese elites in the pre-independence period gave way after independence to competition for access to power. As leaders on both sides manipulated ethnicity to mobilize their political bases, ethnicity became a potent dividing force. Short-sighted state polices in education and employment, aggravated by the government's agenda of "Sinhalization," became the foundation of the Tamil war against the state. The demands of the Tamils spiraled from equal access to education and employment opportunities (1950s–60s), to federalism (1970s), to independence by any means (1980s–90s).

Education and Ethnic Conflict

The Tamils, concentrated in the arid areas of the island, placed great emphasis on education and professional employment (in the civil service, armed forces, medicine, and engineering). Their British rulers encouraged them to seek employment in these fields as a way out of poverty. As a result, by independence, the Tamils were overrepresented in government and the professions relative to their share of Sri Lanka's population. The Sinhalese-dominated government that took over after independence was determined to redress this situation, and the Westminster system instituted at independence enabled them to do so. The system meant that the political parties needed only to court the vote of the Sinhalese majority; their total defeat in the Tamil areas would not affect their electoral fortunes. The Sinhalese political parties therefore engaged in intra-ethnic outbidding, competing with each other to pass laws that favored the Sinhalese and, by extension, hurt the prospects of Tamils in education and employment.

From the 1960s onward, the government instituted legislation that declared Sinhala as the official language of education, professional employment, and government services; announced preferential policies for rural Sinhalese; and required Tamils to score higher than Sinhalese on competitive exams to obtain equal treatment. The Tamils protested peacefully, and the government responded by revising laws to allow for the "reasonable use of Tamil" in education, government correspondence in English, and government service examinations in Tamil for Tamils, although they had to acquire proficiency in Sinhala to be eligible for promotions. But in some cases the revisions took eight years to take effect.

---

[6]For further discussion, see Peris (1991) and DeSilva (1994).

Even when Tamil was given some form of official status, the government made no attempt to link educational structures between the Tamils and Sinhalese at the school and university levels. Free education was given to both communities, but each imparted education in its language and English was not usually taught in the schools. As a result, the two groups were unable to communicate with each other, and lack of interaction reinforced negative historical stereotypes. Ethnocentric associations developed, with few attempts to build associations that bridged differences between groups. In addition to the problems imposed by linguistically segregated education, history textbooks reflected the Sinhalese understanding of history.[7] Tamil teachers consequently rejected these books and interpreted history from the Tamil standpoint. As the conflict gained momentum and the government lost influence in the north and east, the LTTE took on the role of publishing the Tamil version of history textbooks.

Discrimination against Tamils in access to higher education and professional employment continued in different forms, such as quota systems favoring the Sinhalese. The Tamils most affected by these laws were those educated in the 1960s; they were 17–21 years old in 1972, when the conflict turned increasingly violent. This educated class with few employment opportunities formed the backbone of the Tamil movement.[8]

The ethnic divisions within the education structure had long-lasting and dangerous impacts on the organizational structure of educational institutions, training of teachers, and content of textbooks and syllabi. Moreover this segregation was increasingly replicated within other spheres of society, entrenching inter-ethnic hatred even more deeply.

Clearly, education policy in Sri Lanka created a citizenry divided by language with a version of history selected by the state in which there was no place for competing narratives (Rajagopalan 2001). The state became an agent of the Sinhalese community and faced opposition from an increasingly vocal and militant Tamil minority. Even as the conflict gained momentum, education remained highly centralized (until 1987). Not surprisingly, the editorial committees and writers of historical textbooks were Sinhalese. In 2000 in an effort to resolve the conflict, legislation was passed allowing the teaching of Sinhalese in Tamil schools and Tamil in Sinhalese schools, with English as the bridging language. The legislation's impact on relations between the two groups, filled with hatred and anger after a 30-year vicious cycle of violence, is not yet clear.

Applying the Conflict Analysis Framework

Because it plays a critical role in education in most countries, the state can potentially reduce tensions among different ethnic groups through the design of conflict-sensitive education structures. In the case of Sri Lanka, the state did not

---

[7]Among the many works on history in Sri Lankan education, see the early 1980s study on "School Text Books and Communal Relations in Sri Lanka" by the Council of Communal Harmony through the Media, and the 1991 research on "Teaching and Learning Hatred: The Role of Education and Socialization in Sri Lanka" by Sasanka Perera. Rajagopalan (2001) analyzes both studies.

[8]For details on the backgrounds of early leaders, see Swamy 1994.

use the education system to foster tolerance, build social cohesion, and encourage respect for diversity. Instead, from the late 1950s it advanced linguistically segregated education and developed a curriculum that gave primacy to the majority community's interpretation of history, contributing to a population divided along ethnic lines.

The CAF contains several variables that are important in understanding Sri Lanka's conflict dynamics and the implications for government policies and development interventions. Those variables are social and economic cleavages, ethnic cleavages, regional imbalances, horizontal social capital, mythmaking, governance and political institutions, income disparities, employment and access to productive resources (including education), and the role of the diaspora. The critical issue of access to higher education can be analyzed under the subvariable of "differential social opportunities." That variable is the logical anchor for an analysis of the history and the changes that occurred before and after independence, the wider issues that constrain equality in education today, how those issues are likely to develop, and the public attitudes and biases within several subcategories of the two main ethnic groups. Analysis of the variable can further include the important questions about how issues of access to education had been, and may still be, politicized by key players, about the different organizations and groups that have been formed or influenced by this issue, and about how they in turn were able to influence changes in the education sector.

A contextualized conflict analysis applied at an early stage of Sri Lanka's conflict could have underscored how the policy of limiting the minority ethnic group's access to higher education, and thus socioeconomic progress, was contributing to increased ethnic polarization among the Tamil minority. Once ethnic polarization was identified as a risk factor, the conflict analysis could have also drawn attention to the potential and early signs of the emergence of a violent, ethnically based militant movement rallying around a set of grievances to challenge the state. Although in the case of Sri Lanka, education was by no means the only Tamil grievance, the issue of access to education became a highly symbolic rallying point and a key tool in the recruitment of a cadre of militants.

Application of CAF to Sri Lanka could have allowed analysts to focus on several important education-related questions. How and to what extent was education fuelling the conflict? As tensions escalated, was it becoming mainly a symbolic issue, or was it being used as a rallying point to mobilize young people across the country or regions? What were the demographic and economic consequences of the government's education policies, and how were they affecting patterns of poverty and exclusion in the country? A good application of the CAF in Sri Lanka, updated at regular intervals, could have shown that ethnic divisions and animosities in the education sector were manifesting themselves in ways that went beyond visible problems of ethnic access, and instead permeated the organizational structure of education institutions, teacher training, and the content of textbooks and syllabi. Language-based segregation in most schools and universities was increasingly replicated within other socioeconomic spheres, further entrenching ethnic animosity. A deeper analysis of conflict dynamics in the education sector could have pointed to the direct effect of education policies on both conflict and poverty. A large number of young people in minority areas were unable to enroll in higher education despite being qualified academically. Many of them remained unemployed for long periods, and a substantial number of those unemployed were recruited into rebel groups.

The discriminatory education system also had direct effects on poverty. The difficulty of finding qualified teachers in ethnic minority areas negatively affected the quality of education and further limited economic opportunities for young people. Once started, the conflict itself disrupted productive activities, destroyed infrastructure, and limited investment, thereby exacerbating the social, economic, and regional disparities that had sparked the conflict in the first place.

An early application of a CAF-type analysis could have allowed policymakers and development partners to undertake a more careful evaluation of the education policies and programs they were supporting. It could have led policy and program designers to consider the scope for, and feasibility of: restructuring education institutions that were ethno-linguistically segregated (schools, universities, and teacher training institutes); rewriting the ethnically biased contents of textbooks; and training teachers to meet the challenges of a multiethnic and multicultural society. Within such a broad framework of reforms, programs and projects could have further considered ways of involving communities and key stakeholders, as well as the use of innovative technologies to ensure that the education system could better reflect the realities of all ethnic groups and the development of multiple perspectives based on principles of inclusion and social cohesion.

Conclusion

In Sri Lanka, the state did not use the education system to enhance social cohesion in an ethnically divided society. The brief case study of Sri Lanka presented above implies that if some form of conflict analysis—as a more specialized form of social analysis—had been undertaken in the early phases of the conflict, the state could have been alerted to the dangers of implementing a Sinhalese-dominated education system, which many observers argue was a key reason for the acceleration of the violent Tamil insurgency. Furthermore, the government and its development partners could have been prompted to develop education structures that were more inclusive, and curricula and textbooks that were less biased, thus encouraging greater ethnic harmony and national integrative processes. It is not possible to assert that, had this been done, Sri Lanka's violent conflict would have been averted, as there were other important grievances that the LTTE used to mobilize violent opposition against the state. Nevertheless, it is clear that education policies and interventions were not viewed through a conflict-sensitive lens, which could potentially have removed one of the grievances at the source of the conflict, or at least ensured that education policies did not make matters worse. Since the early 1990s, after about two decades of conflict, there has been growing interest in analyzing the influence of education in Sri Lanka's conflict.

The Sri Lankan government has now begun the process of redesigning the education system and revising history textbooks. While education reforms are clearly important to set a solid foundation for peace and postconflict reconstruction, the legacy of conflict and ethnic polarization will require a broader and concerted effort by the government, Sri Lanka's society, and the country's development partners to ensure that postconflict rehabilitation and reconstruction build a more inclusive and cohesive society.

References

Buckland, Peter. 2004. *Reshaping the Future: Education and Post-Conflict Reconstruction.* Washington, DC: World Bank.

DeSilva, K. M. 1994. *The "Traditional Homelands" of the Tamils, Separatist Ideology in Sri Lanka: A Historical Appraisal.* Kandy: Sri Lanka: International Center for Ethnic Studies.

King, E., and Berk Ozler. 1998. "What's Decentralization Got to Do with Learning? The Case of Nicaragua's School Autonomy Reform." Impact Evaluation of Education Reforms Paper 9. World Bank, Development Research Group, Washington, DC.

Peris, C. H. 1991. "An Appraisal of the Concept of Traditional Tamil Homeland in Sri Lanka." *Ethnic Studies Report* IX (1). University of Peradeniya.

Rajagopalan, S. 2001. *State and Nation in South Asia.* Boulder, CO: Lynne Rienner.

Sommers, M., and P. Buckland. 2004. *Parallel Worlds. Rebuilding the Education System.* Paris: International Institute for Educational Planning and World Bank.

Smith, A., and T. Vaux. 2003. *Education, Conflict, and International Development.* London: Department for International Development.

Swamy, N. 1994. *Tigers of Lanka: From Boys to Guerrillas.* Delhi: Konark.

Uemura, Mitsue. 1999. "Community Participation in Education: What Do We Know?" World Bank Working Paper 24670, Washington, DC.

World Bank. 2001. *World Development Report 2000/2001: Attacking Poverty.* NY: Oxford University Press.

———. 2002. "The Conflict Analysis Framework (CAF). Identifying Conflict-related Obstacles to Development." *Conflict Prevention and Reconstruction Unit Dissemination Notes* 5 (September). Conflict Prevention and Reconstruction Unit, Social Development Department, Washington, DC.

———. 2003. *The Role of the World Bank in Conflict and Development: An Evolving Agenda.* Conflict Prevention and Reconstruction Unit, Social Development Department, Washington, DC.

———. 2003b. *Social Analysis Sourcebook: Incorporating Social Dimensions into Bank-Supported Projects.* World Bank, Washington, DC.

———. 2004. "Sector-Specific Guidelines for Social Analysis: Education." Draft. Social Development Department, Washington, DC.

8

Diversity-Sensitive Interventions in Curriculum, Textbooks, and Pedagogical Practices: Guidelines for International Assistance Agencies

James Socknat

Task leaders in international assistance agencies need guidance in assisting countries seeking to promote peace and equitable opportunity in and through their education systems. That was one of the recommendations emerging from the World Bank's March 2003 conference on "Curricula, Textbooks, and Pedagogical Practices and the Promotion of Peace and Respect for Diversity."

The guidelines in this chapter, drafted with specific reference to the World Bank, respond to that recommendation. It is the author's hope that other aid organizations will adapt them for their own use, so that others may benefit from the improvements they make.

Following a short, general discussion of the scope and timing of interventions in education projects, the guidelines in this chapter are divided into separate sections on curriculum, textbooks, and teaching practices. Each section of the guidelines contains a checklist of items to look for when assessing an education system and suggestions for what to do about them.

The task leader's first look at these items will be brief and guided, most likely, by widely known complaints or obviously inappropriate treatment of population groups in the curriculum, textbooks, or teaching practice. During any formal review process, the same items will be considered again in greater detail. The review will suggest actions to be taken; these will depend on myriad country-specific circumstances, notably whether the country is free of immediate conflict, in the midst of conflict, or emerging from conflict.

References in the text to "lender" and "borrower" reflect the genesis of these guidelines in World Bank experience. Readers may wish to substitute the terms "donor" and "recipient."

Degrees of Freedom in Promoting Diversity in Education Systems—Some Dos and Don'ts

Efforts to foster respect for diversity in educational content and practices should be based on a coherent and coordinated review of curriculum, textbooks, and pedagogical practices—followed by necessary revisions in all areas. These steps are in keeping with sound practices for the design of any intervention to introduce new or modified content in the teaching and learning processes. Experience shows that attempts to change the curriculum without making corresponding changes in textbooks and ensuring that teachers are trained and given incentives to teach the new curriculum are likely to fail.[1]

Diversity may be defined narrowly (for example, as referring to ethnic groups) or broadly (gender, language of instruction, religion, and cultural identity, as well as ethnicity). The broader the definition, the larger the array of stakeholders who should be involved in the consultation and review process, and the longer the review, redesign, and retraining are likely to take. The time needed must be balanced against the undesirable phenomenon of sequential reviews and revisions of curriculum, textbooks, and teacher training, and the attendant costs and drain on the time and attention of education officials. The decision on the breadth of review will be influenced by the severity and salience of diversity issues in the society, and by recent history. For example, if gender issues in education were recently reviewed, they may not need to be reviewed again.

Each international assistance agency will have its own rules governing direct involvement in decisions on curriculum, textbook content, and pedagogical practices. However, we expect that most agencies will have a similar approach to that of the World Bank in terms of direct involvement of staff in the review.

Reviews of curriculum content, textbooks, and pedagogic practice should not be undertaken directly by development agency or donor staff. Even if the staff had the resources to conduct such a review, most donors would not wish to put themselves in the position of telling client countries what does or does not promote tolerance and diversity. Thus, such a review would be inappropriate in sector work (to use the Bank's parlance) or analytical or advisory activities.

What the Bank and other donors *can* do is to provide financial support under a lending operation (project) to conduct such a review under the direction of the borrower and to provide technical assistance for appropriate revisions in curriculum, textbooks, and teaching practices as flagged in the review.[2]

As a general rule, the World Bank will not *insist* that countries launch a review of curriculum, textbooks, and pedagogical practices to foster respect for diversity. However, the staff can raise this review as representing good practice (see below). They can also present evidence of the economic benefits of tolerance and respect for diversity. This economic rationale may be included in the policy dialogue between the Bank and the borrower.

In rare cases, the curriculum, textbook contents, or pedagogical practices may be so egregious that they are a source of open dispute between one or more subpopulations and the government. In these rare instances, agency staff may consider requiring that governments establish a review process as a condition for assistance.[3]

Many countries can benefit from the opportunity to hear from organizations that have experience in setting up processes for the review of curriculum, text-

---

[1]In addition, in countries where "high stakes" examinations certify students' completion of a stage of education or determine their eligibility for the next, the examination must include some questions from the new or revised curriculum. If it does not, teachers are unlikely to teach the material, and students are unlikely to focus on it.

[2]No Bank staff member should serve on the review panel.

[3]The danger of insisting on a review is that the borrower might not feel sufficient ownership to carry it out with full vigor and enthusiasm. On the other hand, the consequences of not pushing the borrower toward a review in extreme cases may be damage to the Bank's reputation. In such circumstances, the potential deficit of ownership is clearly the lesser evil.

books, and pedagogical practices. Two such organizations are the Georg Eckert Institute for International Textbook Research in Braunschweig, Germany, and the University of Ulster, Northern Ireland. These organizations can provide advisory assistance on structuring the review process, train government staff and prospective review panelists, and organize study tours to allow country representatives to meet and hear directly from participants in reviews carried out in other countries.

When to Intervene

Those involved in reviews of educational content and practices that initiatives will succeed only if launched during a "window of opportunity." Typically, these windows open up in postconflict situations, when the disputing factions have abandoned conflict and formed a government committed to reconciliation and reunification. In the early stage of this new government, memories of the high price of conflict are fresh, so there is a willingness to try a new approach. An initiative to review curriculum, textbooks, and teaching practices has a high chance of success during this crucial period, provided champions for the effort can be found.

Other windows of opportunity may occur when the society is opening to democracy, or when the government is making commitments to rectify long-standing social inequities. In the early stages of such sociopolitical change, the government has a mandate to address social exclusions and sources of protracted poverty. That mandate should increase the government's willingness to try new approaches to old problems. The broad vision of a new, more open society can produce champions of efforts to foster respect for diversity and more pluralistic participation in social and economic life.

Preventive interventions to ensure that curricula, textbooks, and pedagogical practices encourage respect for diversity can succeed in societies not embroiled in open conflict. When the situation is calm, there may be great chances for rational discussion and appropriate action.

A fourth type of window may open when a government makes a commitment to improve the quality of education, as in the Lao PDR, Peru, and Sri Lanka (all underpinned by World Bank loan agreements). In such situations, it may be legitimate for Bank staff to ask whether proposed quality improvements are sensitive to diversity. Why? Because inclusive education draws on a larger pool of talent and therefore promotes economic and social development.

An initiative to foster respect for diversity when conflict is still in progress is unlikely to get off the ground. What *can* be done in some situations of ongoing conflict is to provide training for future champions of the respect-for-diversity review process. Bilateral international assistance agencies and NGOs may be better positioned than the World Bank to provide such training, given the conditions necessary for World Bank assistance.

In countries not immersed in conflict, Bank staff may consider supporting a review sought by the government—because, in education as in health, *preventive measures generally are more cost effective than remedial efforts*. Before doing so, however, they should ensure that critical groups in the country are understood fully and that the country has champions who are ready to lead the review and to implement its recommendations. Their assessment should cover social, institutional, and economic conditions in the country. To borrow conclusions and approaches from other countries generally is misleading and could be seriously counterproductive. By contrast, a review process carried out by appropriate national representatives of relevant stakeholder groups is likely to have better local insight and understanding of the various critical groups. In addition, such a group may be less tempted to borrow inappropriately from reviews in other countries.

Governments that embark on a respect-for-diversity initiative usually need help in reaching out to the media to explain the objectives of the initiative, provide examples of the problems that would be avoided, and demonstrate the benefits that would be obtained. Failure to communicate in advance with the media may result in media attacks that could damage, or even destroy, the initiative.

Any initiative in the areas of curriculum, textbooks, and pedagogical practices should be audited for effectiveness. The project of which the initiative is a part should include plans, and funds, for monitoring and assessing progress. It is particularly important that the Ministry of Education should acquire the capacity to collect and analyze evidence of the teaching and learning outcomes of the respect-for-diversity initiative.

Curriculum—What to Do and How

Coordinate Revisions

Because revising a curriculum is expensive and time consuming, it is irresponsible to recommend to governments that revisions be made frequently and without regard for the implications—notably the cost of new textbooks required and of training teachers to be able to deliver the new curriculum. Depending on the country's policy for providing textbooks and on their physical specifications, textbooks may last from one to four years. Specifications that allow three or four years of book life are the most economical—some one-third of the unit cost of a book designed to last only one year. If curricula are changed more frequently than three or four years, either the textbooks will not match the curricula, or the cost-effectiveness of the textbook provision strategy will have been undermined.

Where there are multiple requests for curriculum revisions (for example, to improve gender sensitivity, pay greater attention to environmental issues, and raise HIV/AIDS awareness) the sensible approach is to handle all of the revision objectives in the same process. However, this general truth must be tempered by the complexity of the task. Pragmatism may dictate that only certain revisions, and not others, can be made during a single round of revision of curriculum.

Integrate Diversity Throughout the Curriculum

As a general principle, respect for diversity should be well integrated throughout the curriculum. Treating it as a special subject can segregate it, unless the content is complemented throughout the curriculum by the manner in which students are taught, how classrooms are organized, the holiday calendar, and the behaviors encouraged in students, teachers, and school administration. In some cases, it may be useful to prototype curriculum changes in particular schools, as the first stage of systemwide reform. For example, the East Bay Conservation Corps School, a charter school in the United States that serves a poor area with troubled youth, integrates respect for diversity and service learning (civic engagement) throughout its curriculum.

Involve Stakeholders

When the curriculum is being revised to foster tolerance and respect for diversity, it is good practice to encourage the government to appoint an advisory committee with representatives of all relevant stakeholders, particularly ethnic and religious groups. The transparency of a process with broad stakeholder involvement is likely to generate significant political capital for the government. Some argue that rather than an advisory committee or advisory board, the government should establish a panel of "critical friends." Obtaining proactive input and feedback from minority groups and other relevant stakeholders early in the revision process is much more sensible and cost effective than revising the curriculum, piloting it, and then getting reactions from society. It is especially important that the stakeholders enlisted to participate in the review be asked to identify the aspects of the curriculum that have caused resentment and tension. In other words, the advisory committee or panel of "critical friends" should be asked not only to review proposed solutions, but also to help identify problems and provide advice during the curriculum development process.

Securing stakeholder participation and engagement from the outset is crucial. Many national governments have underestimated the effort and planning that this commitment actually involves. Governments' "participation" efforts often have been token exercises that involved a few press releases or pamphlets to parents, rather than true engagement of representatives from diverse groups over a sustained period (sometimes several years).

In the establishment of advisory or review panels, it is useful to enlist expertise from outside of the education community to benefit from the fresh views that they can bring to the process.

If at all possible, the project should include support that will enable national teams working on curriculum revision to be linked across countries into communities of practitioners. To ensure coordination and coherence of the three elements of the initiative, a member of the team working on the curriculum dimension of the initiative also should serve on the textbooks team. Another member of the curriculum team should serve on the pedagogical practices team.

School principals and senior staff have an important role in leading diversity initiatives. Those leading the review should consider how best to involve senior staff in the process of curriculum review and clarify their role in supporting and implementing change. Two main issues must be dealt with. The first is the degree of diversity within the senior staff of the education system—because internal diversity sends strong messages to those working in schools about the value placed on diversity by the education authorities. The second issue is the extent to which senior staff understand and support proposed curriculum change and the development of diversity-sensitive pedagogies. If deficits are detected, management training may be called for.

Once the curriculum initiative has been designed, it is important for the government to raise awareness among publishers, so that they understand the curriculum reforms that will need to be reflected in new textbooks.

State the Aims of the Review

The government should state the central aims of the new curriculum and invite a debate on that statement. Most curricula reflect some compromise among three views:

- Those who see education as mainly about *personal and moral development* and are likely to see its aims in terms of the value of learning for the individual
- Those who see education as mainly about *social and cultural development* and are likely to be more concerned with learning processes and cultural reproduction
- Those who see education as mainly about *economic development* and are likely to emphasize transmission of technical knowledge and vocational education.

These are simplifications and are not mutually exclusive, but rarely do governments initiate public debate about the resolution of emphasis on personal, social, or economic development. Therefore, the proposed new curriculum often becomes a battleground among proponents of particular subject disciplines, rather than proposals for balanced provision in each area. In particular, it is rare for government to articulate the economic as well as the social benefits of inclusive (diversity-sensitive) education.

Specify the Type of Curriculum Being Proposed

Internationally, there is considerable rhetoric about the need to move toward skills-based, rather than content-based curricula. Various arguments are put forward to support this shift. (See, for example, chapter 2 in this volume.) They include the realization that because knowledge is increasing exponentially, it is not possible to revise curricula quickly enough to keep pace with advances. Nor is it possible simply to add more and more content to already crowded syllabi. The significant shift, therefore, is toward specifying the content of syllabi in terms of transferable skills and learning outcomes, rather than facts and figures to be learned and reproduced in examinations. Nevertheless, the latter statement describes the reality in most countries.

A genuine shift toward a skills-based curriculum has huge implications for all aspects of curriculum change, organization of the education system, and deployment of resources. It suggests an inquiry-based approach to teaching and learning in which the starting point is to pose problems for pupils to investigate. It assumes that pupils have access to a diverse range of resources, know how to access them, and have the capacity to make value judgments about the reliability and credibility of various sources and types of evidence. It implies a view of the role of the teacher as a facilitator of learning rather than a gatekeeper of knowledge. This view, in turn, has implications for the recruitment and training of teachers. It also has implications for the assessment of learning and the setting of national examinations.

Some would argue that a commitment to move toward a skills-based curriculum has a greater potential to effect fundamental change—by developing transferable skills for economic as well as social development—than any number of revisions and changes to the content of various subject areas. The promise of skills-based curricula for the development of greater sensitivity to diversity may be:

- A realization by learners that many aspects of knowledge are "intersubjective," that is, they are shared by a group of people (for understandable reasons) but are not universal or absolutely and objectively true
- Development of skills of critical inquiry, openness, cooperation, and empathy for diverse perspectives
- Use of multiple sources of evidence
- Willingness and ability of teachers to challenge pupils' values.

Task managers from donor groups can facilitate, encourage, and support their country counterparts in grappling with these challenging questions about the *aims* and *type* of the curriculum they are trying to introduce, based on the view that genuine inquiry-based curricula may be more consistent with the development of skills that are sensitive to diversity.

In certain countries where the government lacks the resources to fully implement change, nongovernmental organizations (NGOs) may be an integral element of the strategy for curriculum development (Jagannathan 2001). In such cases, the NGOs may be regarded as full partners, with responsibility for implementing particular aspects of the curriculum review process, such as dissemination of a specific methodology and pedagogy. Task managers might help education authorities undertake an audit of NGOs to identify their particular strengths and draw up a short list of those that might be partners in the curriculum process. Support may also be required to eventually scale up pilot initiatives initially undertaken by NGOs.

Checklist on Curriculum

What to Look For

✓ *What are the stated aims of the curriculum?*

Are they mainly about reproduction of the majority cultural values, nation building, or economic development? Might it be possible to include a statement about the value of diversity? One might say, for example, that sensitivity to diversity is important in developing a shared sense of belonging or that an inclusive approach to education can contribute to economic development by minimizing grievances that threaten security, by drawing on the full talent within a society, by creating the social skills for an integrated workforce.

✓ *What type of curriculum is being proposed?*

Is it about critical inquiry and the development of transferable skills, or about the transmission of facts and figures for their own sake? To what extent does the curriculum pose questions, and how relevant are those questions to the social, cultural, and economic challenges that the country faces? Do the education authorities recognize the significance of a change to a skills-based curriculum and its implications for investment in areas of resources, pedagogy, teacher education, and assessment? What specific changes are planned in each of these areas?

✓ *Is the coverage of the country's history and culture:*

- . . . Complete? Does it deal with gender, religion, and ethnicity in its treatment of the country's population groups?

- . . . Balanced? Is the curriculum balanced in the way it allocates time and objectives to the country's various population groups? Do the curriculum objectives emphasize national pride to the exclusion of the value of peace?
- . . . In context? Does the curriculum place the country's history and culture in a regional and international context? Does it contain selective or unbalanced treatments of relations with neighboring or other countries? Does it distort the history or culture of neighboring or other countries?

✓ *Which diversity-related issues are most salient in the society?*

Are some diversity issues acute in comparison with others? For example, is ethnicity a major problem? Religion? In the last several years, has the curriculum been reviewed for its treatment of any particular population group? If so, how were relevant population groups represented in the review process?

What to Do

✓ *Identify the key actors in the curriculum review process.*

Look beyond ministry officials to a range of stakeholders. Then support them as they confront questions about the aims of the curriculum and consider the links between sensitivity to diversity and positive social and economic development.

✓ *Create a working link with the Ministry of Education.*

Be sure an appropriate representative of the education ministry is assigned to oversee the review process and has the technical competence to manage the process within the specified timeframe.

✓ *Help key actors develop a clear view of the type of curriculum at which they are aiming.*

Assist them in gaining access to international networks of curriculum authorities and agencies; sources of practical experience with country-specific curriculum review processes; examples of how various aspects of diversity (gender, language of instruction, inclusion of minorities, and recognition of different cultures in curriculum content) have been addressed in other countries' curricula.

✓ *Allow ample time for planning.*

Be realistic about the time it takes to accomplish the foregoing tasks. Hint: It's usually longer than you think.

✓ *Determine the scope of the review.*

Key areas of the curriculum that seem to come up in many different countries include: gender; language of instruction; inclusion of minorities (a relative term that varies depending on the local context); provision for religion; inclusion of diverse material related to cultural development in subject areas such as art, literature, music, sports; teaching history, geography, civics, and citizenship; and the extent to which the curriculum includes human rights education to meet government's commitments to international instruments. Task managers may wish to flag these subject areas to their country counterparts in the ministry of education.

✓ *Look for champions and windows of opportunity*

Can you detect a window of opportunity for a review of the curriculum with respect to one or more diversity issues? Can you find a champion for the idea of a curriculum review?

✓ *Settle on the composition of the review panel.*

If it appears to be appropriate to proceed with a review, what panel composition seems most appropriate? National panelists only? International panelists only? A combination of national and international panelists?

- Who should be included as members of the review committee?
- How will representation of the relevant population groups in the review process be determined? (Choices are not mutually exclusive.)
- What is the process for obtaining feedback from relevant population groups?

Textbooks—What to Do and How

The textbook component of a respect-for-diversity initiative must be designed in the context of the country's overall textbook policy and practices. Begin by situating the country on the publication spectrum. That spectrum extends from full state authorship, publishing, and printing to a limited state role that may including setting the criteria for textbooks and establishing a list of books from which schools may choose. Where the state's role is not all-inclusive, private publishers will produce the textbooks.

World Bank staff working on a respect-for-diversity initiative with a textbook element should consult "World Bank Operational Guidelines for Textbooks and Reading Materials" (World Bank 2002) and the Bank's standard bidding document on "Procurement of Textbooks and Reading Materials" (World Bank 2003).

Producing a new textbook takes years. So be realistic in setting timetables for the initiative. A rule of thumb is to allow two years between the call for new textbooks (accompanied by criteria and specifications) and delivery of printed books. This time can vary depending on the extent of field testing. Writing the textbook should not begin until the curriculum review and revisions have been completed. However, capacity building in the Ministry of Education and in the country's publishing industry can—and often should—be started before the call for new textbooks is issued.

If the initiative is to have maximum impact, textbooks should be accompanied by new teachers' manuals and other materials. How problem-solving groups and practical exercises are structured and conducted can be as important as texts and illustrations that do not stereotype, insult, or ignore various population groups.

When distance learning is, or could be, used, materials for distance learning as well as traditional textbooks need to be prepared.

Transparency is essential in any textbook initiative. The media relations program suggested in a preceding section can help, as can setting out very carefully and clearly the criteria for improving respect for diversity in textbooks.

Further suggestions on design and implementation of the textbook component of a respect-for-diversity initiative may be found in the *UNESCO Guidebook on Textbook Research and Textbook Revision* (Pingel 2002).

Checklist on Textbooks

What to Look For

✓ *What is the present process for producing textbooks?*

Who currently commissions authors, publishes and distributes textbooks? How do these arrangements affect the diversity-sensitivity of the texts produced? Does the overall process—not only the content but also the *commissioning, writing, production, and publishing*—include diverse groups, authors, and vendors?

✓ *Do current textbooks do justice to all groups in society?*

Do they provide adequate and balanced coverage of relevant ethnic, religious, and gender groups? Is the treatment in textbooks respectful of all groups? Are any population groups stereotyped in the textbooks? Do the textbooks overuse terminology familiar only to particular population groups? Do the textbooks use words or phrases that convey a particular group's perspective on history, culture, and national life?

✓ *Are some diversity issues much more severe than others? For example, does the treatment in a textbook of one particular ethnic group seem especially contentious?*

Has there been a recent review of textbooks for treatment of any particular population group, such as a particular religion? If so, what representatives of the relevant population group were part of the review process?

✓ *Do the textbooks fairly and accurately describe current and past relations with neighboring countries, without derogatory or inflammatory references?*

Do the textbook illustrations and artwork portray other groups in stereotypical or negative ways? Do they accurately portray the attire and behavior of neighboring groups? Do textbook maps accurately depict current or past national boundaries, especially in the context of current or past territorial disputes?

✓ *Are there teachers' manuals for the various textbooks, and do they provide guidance on how to handle alternative perspectives on and interpretations of national history and culture?*

What to Do

✓ *Support a review of the arrangements for the commissioning, authoring, publishing, and distributing textbooks to consider how more diversity-sensitive processes might be established.*

✓ *Look for champions and windows of opportunity.*

Can you detect a window of opportunity for a review of textbooks for diversity issues? Is there a logical champion for the idea of a review?

✓ *Settle on the composition of the review panel.*

If it appears to be appropriate to proceed with a review, what panel composition seems most appropriate? National panelists only? International panelists only? A combination of national and international panelists?

- Who should be included as members of the review committee?
- How will representation of the relevant population groups in the review process be determined? (Choices are not mutually exclusive.)
- What is the process for obtaining feedback from relevant population groups?

✓ *If the country has a history of conflict with one or more neighbors, ask whether a joint review of the countries' textbooks to detect derogatory or inflammatory material might be timely or feasible.*

Pedagogical Practices—What to Do and How

A new curriculum and new textbooks may have no appreciable impact unless teachers know how to put them to their intended uses. Therefore, a successful respect-for-diversity initiative must contain a component on pedagogical practices. That component should extend into several areas of the education system, as discussed below.

Recruitment of Teachers

In an inclusive education system, one would expect the teaching corps to reflect the broader society. For that reason, it is important to determine, at an early stage, the demographic pattern of teachers already working within the system. This research is likely to highlight gaps and deficiencies in the supply of teachers such as gender imbalance, difficulties in recruitment due to low pay and status, and difficulties in recruiting for rural areas.

Determining the profile of the current teaching corps also will bring to light other difficulties that directly affect sensitivity to diversity within the school system. These may include the lack of mother-tongue teachers for children from certain minorities, underrepresentation of particular ethnic groups among teachers, and lower qualifications among certain groups that impede their entry in the teaching profession.

Teacher supply and demand are long-term issues that can be addressed only through a long-term recruitment plan. Imaginative strategies and interventions will be needed to address lack of diversity. These measures can be controversial, but such plans need to be initiated sooner rather than later. Otherwise, the lack of diversity in existing patterns likely will be replicated from one generation to the next. Again, educating teachers, parents, and the public in advance for these changes will smooth the way.

Initial Teacher Education

The pattern of initial teacher education may reflect structural biases, such as inaccessibility for rural or minority groups or the maintenance of separate teacher-training institutions for different linguistic, religious, or ethnic groups. Where separate institutions exist, there is a particular challenge to provide trainees with an awareness of and exposure to a diversity of cultures, traditions, and beliefs. Such exposure can be achieved by making diversity awareness part of the teacher-training curriculum and by ensuring that trainees come into contact with other traditions and beliefs. That can be done by inviting representatives to the college to speak, making contact with a variety of external institutions, and providing opportunities for trainees and new teachers to practice in schools of a different tradition.

Where there are common teacher education institutions, the challenge is to draw on the diversity that exists internally as a teaching resource (rather than assuming that students automatically will develop intercultural awareness). In countries that lack a well-developed system for teacher education, prospective teachers are likely to be drawn from school-leavers who have completed nine or ten years of education, or even less. Armed with few qualifications, new teachers will be sent directly into classrooms. Their formal "training" may consist of an apprenticeship with existing teachers; more likely, new teachers simply will replicate the teaching styles of the teachers who taught them.

In all these situations, the key question is how the teacher-training curriculum can be used to impart pedagogies and practices that are sensitive to diversity. Several related factors will shape the answer to that question, among them the following:

- The degree of diversity on the faculty of the teachers' college, the awareness of that faculty of diversity issues, and the teaching pedagogies that they model to trainee teachers.
- The opportunities that teacher trainees have to draw on their own experiences of diversity (if any), to have their own values challenged, and to practice diversity-sensitive teaching methods. Teachers need to understand that they may not be aware of their own biases and to recognize that noncurricular and non-subject-specific aspects of education can foster prejudice and bias (for example, illustrations and classroom wall hangings, seating arrangements, use of language, songs, and even sports). Most trainees could benefit from group sensitivity sessions with a skilled facilitator in which they can share and work through their personal feelings about diversity issues to gain a more tolerant and supportive perspective.
- Opportunities for intercultural learning and an introductory course on human rights values and principles as an element of every initial teacher education course. Experiences from respect-for-diversity initiatives also suggest that teacher education and training should include mandatory courses on local traditions, diversity, and its importance. Every teacher should be trained in mediation and conflict resolution.

In-Service Professional Development

Teachers' in-service professional development poses challenges similar to those of initial teacher education, with two notable exceptions. First, serving teachers have already have built up a repertoire of teaching methods that may or may not be sensitive to diversity. Second, the extent to which serving teachers are open to change may vary. Several strategies can help build their awareness of diversity:

School-based development. The strength of school-based strategies is that they allow school staff to meet collectively to address diversity issues facing the whole school. Those issues may include an analysis of the communities served by the school; how pupils can be introduced to a wider range of cultures, traditions, and beliefs; the values that school policies, practices, and staff behaviors communicate to pupils; and school processes to encourage pupil participation in decisions that affect them. School-based professional development also provides opportunities for staff to analyze how sensitive the school environment is to diversity (symbols, displays) and identify how particular subject areas contribute to an awareness of diversity.

Classroom-based strategies can help teachers develop practices that are sensitive to diversity. There is an emerging literature in this area, much of it distilling what essentially are principles of good teaching: securing pupils' engagement through active learning; drawing on pupils' own environment and experiences; making sure all pupil contributions are encouraged and valued; providing opportunities to extend pupils' contact with diverse cultures, traditions, and beliefs; and modeling values of respect for difference and nonviolent behaviors. Some systems appoint education advisors to encourage good practice within the system, although it is rare for them to operate routinely at the level of classroom practice. Other systems rely on school inspection for access to practice at the classroom level, but this inspection usually is part of a monitoring process rather than a means of encouraging new practices. A more progressive approach might involve teachers in peer observation (typically, one on one) and reflection on practice (preferably with a supervisor), although peer observation requires a degree of trust that often is missing in schools.

Center-based courses are a common way for a ministry of education to provide in-service professional development for teachers. This approach brings together teachers from different schools to consider a particular issue. The ability to assemble a diverse group of teachers creates an opportunity in itself, and may also be an effective way of disseminating helpful pedagogies. However, one weakness of this approach may be lack of support to sustain change in practice on returning to the school environment.

Teacher clusters and peer education initiatives may be helpful ways to encourage and sustain pedagogical practices that are sensitive to diversity. Programs for *mentoring* teachers and facilitating *networks* of teachers offer an ongoing way for teachers to provide advice and suggestions to one another, tackle problems as they arise, and grow their repertoire of teaching materials and techniques. The value of such programs lies in the credibility and sharing of experience. Such networks themselves may be structures to provide serving teachers with more diverse experiences and contact with professionals beyond their own communities.

NGOs often have resources and experience that may be lacking within the formal education system and can be an important component of an overall strategy to develop greater sensitivity to diversity. Teachers may look to NGOs to provide insight into diversity issues through the personnel or programs they provide. NGOs often will have very specific expertise in areas related to diverse traditions, cultures, and beliefs that otherwise would be inaccessible to the school.

Professional associations and teachers' unions have an important role in supporting the introduction of practices supportive of diversity. This role can take the form of policy statements supported by the membership, public statements of support for changes in teaching methods, funding of pilot initiatives, and, crucially, participation in working groups as a key stakeholder group.

Timing the implementation of the pedagogic practice element of the respect-for-diversity initiative can be challenging. Typically, textbook revision follows completion of the curriculum revision, and teacher training often is scheduled only after the new textbooks are available. Teacher training, of course, can be launched earlier, especially if the training objective is to raise awareness of teachers about the objectives and timeline of the initiative. In fact, it is critical that teachers be brought on board *as early as possible* to support the initiative.

Training in mediation and conflict resolution and on how to foster respect for diversity through classroom behavior can be carried out while the curriculum and textbook elements of the initiative are under preparation. Eventually, teacher training will be required to ensure that teachers understand the revised curriculum and new textbooks.

The pedagogical element of the initiative should be strongly linked to the curriculum and textbook elements. Having team members from the curriculum and textbook teams on the pedagogical practices team is one way of providing the needed linkage.

Broader community support for changes

New teaching practices may be confusing for parents, particularly if they differ significantly from their own school experience. More participatory methodologies may appear threatening, especially if they seem to challenge established power relations between teachers and pupils and place less emphasis on discipline and control. Education authorities may need to develop strategies to communicate with parents and the wider community about the benefits and reasons for a move toward pedagogies that are more sensitive to diversity. Such strategies might include open days to explain and discuss possible changes, opportunities for parents to observe or participate in lessons, and information campaigns involving various types of media and community forums. Outreach can reduce the risk of the community undermining the school's effort. Moreover, the involvement of parents and the community in the teaching/learning process can reinforce efforts to make teachers more sensitive to diversity in their day-to-day teaching.

Checklist on Pedagogical Practices

What to look for

✓ *Do some diversity issues appear more severe that others?*

For example, do teacher practices regarding classroom participation of one particular ethnic group seem especially contentious? Has there been a recent review of teachers' practices for treatment of any particular population group? (An example might be girls' participation in science classes.) If so, which relevant population groups participated in the review process, and how were they represented?

✓ *How inclusive and sensitive to diversity is the initial teacher education system? Consider institutions, location, staffing, and enrollment.*

✓ *What is the level of understanding of diversity issues among the staff of teacher education institutions?*

✓ *Do preservice courses for teachers include:*

- . . . Awareness raising and guidance for handling diversity issues?
- . . . Training on becoming aware of personal bias?
- . . . Training in human rights values and principles and in the use of conflict management techniques, especially among various student groups?

✓ *What models of in-service education exist in the system?*

Can they be adapted to develop greater sensitivity to diversity? What capacity exists among the staff responsible for in-service education to develop greater personal sensitivity to diversity? Do in-service courses for teachers include:

- . . . Awareness raising and guidance for handling diversity issues?
- . . . Training on becoming aware of personal bias?
- . . . Training in human rights values and principles and in the use of conflict management techniques, especially among various student groups?

✓ *What degree of diversity exists in the senior management of the system?*
Do senior staff understand the importance of diversity? Are there plans to involve senior staff in implementing and supporting changes in pedagogy?

✓ *In the classroom . . .*

Do classroom decorations, wall hangings, and teaching illustrations foster prejudice, bias, or stereotyping? Do teachers call on or otherwise encourage participation of all students, or are there patterns of "favored" groups being called on or encouraged to participate?

✓ *What expertise and strengths exist among NGOs to support the development of teaching methods sensitive to diversity?*

✓ *Are there plans to raise awareness among parents and the wider community about the need for teaching methods sensitive to diversity?*

What to Do

✓ *Support a review of teacher supply and demand that is sensitive to diversity issues.*

Draw on local expertise to complete the review, and provide additional technical support if necessary.

✓ *Look for champions and windows of opportunity.*

Is there a window of opportunity for a review of teaching practices from the perspective of diversity? Can a champion for the idea of a review be found? Does support exist for a review of initial teacher education from a diversity perspective, including structural review of institutional provision, staffing, and enrollment?

✓ *Settle on the composition of the review panel.*

If it appears to be appropriate to proceed with a review, what panel composition seems most appropriate? National panelists only? International panelists only? A combination of national and international panelists? Panelists need not be exclusively teacher trainers and should include representatives of the relevant population groups.

- Who should be included as members of the review committee?
- How will representation of the relevant population groups in the review process be determined? (Choices are not mutually exclusive.)
- Will those representatives serve on the review committee? If not, how will feedback from relevant population groups be obtained?

✓ *Identify opportunities to develop diversity-sensitive pedagogies in initial teacher education courses and assess the capacity of faculty to implement them.*

Find opportunities to pilot innovative practices in initial teacher education to encourage greater exposure to diversity. Examples might include staff exchanges or teaching practice in schools of different traditions.

✓ *Support efforts by education authorities to develop a plan for in-service education.*

The plan should include professional development on a whole-school basis, through classroom practice, and through center-based courses. Support initiatives to strengthen the capacity of staff responsible for in-service development.

✓ *Help education authorities assess the strengths of various NGOs to undertake the development of diversity-sensitive pedagogies.*

Provide funding for agreed pilot initiatives undertaken by NGOs that have strategic importance, and develop a plan to scale up the most successful initiatives.

✓ *Support the development of a plan to involve parents and the community in the introduction of diversity-sensitive pedagogies to schools.*

References

Jagannathan, Shanti. 2001. "The Role of Nongovernmental Organizations in Primary Education: A Study of Six NGOs in India." World Bank Working Paper 2530, Washington, DC.

Pingel, Falk. 2002. "UNESCO Guidebook on Textbook Research and Textbook Revision." Prepared in collaboration with the Georg Eckert Institute for International Textbook Revision. UNESCO document number ED-99/WS/27, Paris.

World Bank. 2002. "World Bank Operational Guidelines for Textbooks and Reading Materials." Working Paper 24693. Washington, DC. Available online from http://www.worldbank.com/reference/.

World Bank. 2003. "Procurement of Textbooks and Reading Materials, Trial Edition." A World Bank standard bidding document. Available online from the Procurement section of www.worldbank.org.